RACE AND REALITY

A SEARCH FOR SOLUTIONS

RACE AND REALITY

A SEARCH FOR SOLUTIONS

By Carleton Putnam

Author of "Race And Reason"

Public Affairs Press, Washington, D. C.

Published by Public Affairs Press
419 New Jersey Ave., S.E., Washington, D. C. 20003

Printed in the United States of America
Library of Congress Catalog Card Number 67-19407

"The great difficulty we have in facing the race problem is that a whole generation of educated Americans have grown up under Professor Boas' teachings. . . . These are the people who are now in power in the United States and they don't know what it's all about. . . . That leaves the race question to be solved only by the more uneducated people in the country. That means it's going to be solved in a pragmatic way which is always, of course, the most disagreeable way possible."
—*Extract from a confidential letter to the author from the son of a former President of the United States.*

CONTENTS

CHAPTER I

MIDNIGHT IN MAINE

Along the coast of Maine in September there are days when the air is like wine and the sky is an infinite blue. One searches for symbols of clarity to describe such days, for they lend themselves to wide vistas across the land and within the mind. Moreover, on Mt. Desert Island a man is on an eastern frontier where he can still find detachment from crowds and controversies, a sense of sanctuary and an inducement to meditation.

On some nights the stars are as bright as the stars of Arizona. I remember such an evening at Seal Harbor in 1966 when I was on a vacation from the debates and contention which had persisted since the publication of my *Race and Reason: A Yankee View* in 1961. It was a tempting night to review and to ponder.

The inducement was doubled by an isolated study, an open fire and a brief case stuffed with papers. So I pondered in the study and fed the fire, trying meanwhile to distill some meaning from the experiences of half a decade. I had closed *Race and Reason* in a contemplative mood—a mood of recapitulation—and now I wondered if the time had not arrived to evaluate the intervening years.

Were I to write the first book over again, what would I change? As for its basic thesis, all that I had said had been validated in the period since it appeared. The passage of Civil Rights Acts, the pro-Negro pressures of government departments and the Negro-oriented stance of the opinion-forming agencies of our society had only resulted in increasing racial tensions throughout the country. Disorders in Philadelphia, New York, Rochester, Cleveland, Los Angeles and other cities were symptomatic of a seething hostility beneath the surface everywhere.

In the Deep South, twelve years after the Supreme Court's school integration decision, less than four per cent of the Negro population were in integrated schools, and these only after threats

1

and bribery from the federal government. In no state had the averages reached more than 15 per cent of the total school enrollment, the flash-point at which trouble could really be expected to start.

In Negro Africa the deterioration had approached the ludicrous. During the sixty days prior to January 1, 1966, five "democratic" African governments—Upper Volta, the Central African Republic, Dahomey, Nigeria and the Congo—were overthrown by force. Since 1960 there had been at least 24 African rebellions, mutinies, assassinations or attempted assassinations, and coup d'etats. Under such circumstances it was not surprising that while the crime rate was rising in the United States cannibalism and human sacrifice were increasing in Africa.

As regards these developments I could only feel that my errors had been more those of omission than commission. There was much documentation I would now add, and there were insights I lacked then and had gained since. Beyond these, there were questions of emphasis. I had underestimated certain forces and overestimated others. The larger framework in which the Negro problem arose was of more importance than I had thought. The relationship of race to the leftward movement on the world stage was closer, the reasons for the dishonesty in this area were clearer. Personal experience with the extent to which otherwise rational people were willing to be deceived had surprised me, but not as much as the lengths to which public leaders, scholars, churchmen, and the mass media would go to alter the fabric of our society in the deception's name.

Throwing another log on the fire, I realized that I was now more aware of these things than I had been five years before. Yet in the interval I had come to appreciate many of them and had taken such limited action as I could at the time. Especially in the area of science and the biology of race differences I had grown familiar with the evasions and other tactics of the educational hierarchy, their blind dedication to the political dogma of equality, and had done my best to expose them.

For example, in my hand I held a newspaper clipping regarding an attack upon Dr. Wesley C. George [1]—author of *The Biology of the Race Problem* and a leading exponent of the truth concerning genetic variability—which served to illustrate the general situation. I paused to re-read it now, and to conjure back some of the incidents that made the episode still vivid in my mind.

The American Anthropological Association had held its annual meeting in November of 1961 and at its final session, at which 192 of the 600 Fellows of the Association were present, unanimously passed a resolution which was later used repeatedly as if it finally disposed of all of Dr. George's work and of *Race and Reason* as well. This resolution read in part: "The American Anthropological Association repudiates statements now appearing in the United States that Negroes are biologically and in innate mental ability inferior [sic] [2] to whites . . ."

The fallacy here was so transparent, so contrary to all the established facts, and yet so likely to mislead an uninformed public on a matter vital to the national welfare that I could not ignore it. To anyone who had studied the background and motives of the leaders in these groups it was stark ideological propaganda without any scientific basis whatever. Moreover, if our domestic and foreign policies were to be bottomed on such blatant inversions of the truth, little hope remained for either a law-abiding or a peaceful world.

Therefore, upon learning of the resolution, I called a press conference in which I publicly asked the retiring president of the Association (a Harvard man) a question I had transmitted to him privately in advance. This question was: Do you also intend to repudiate the following statement by your recently deceased Harvard colleague Professor Clyde Kluckhohn, a Viking Medal winner

---

1. Wesley C. George, Ph.D., Professor of Histology and Embryology, emeritus, and for ten years head of the Department of Anatomy, University of North Carolina Medical School; past president, North Carolina Academy of Science.

2. The choice of the word "inferior" to arouse anger rather than reason among readers or listeners is characteristic of the equalitarian. Phrases such as "limitations of capacity" or "a race younger on the evolutionary scale" are available but avoided by them.

and a long-time equalitarian,[3] who said shortly before he died:
"In the light of accumulating information as to significantly varying incidence of mapped genes among different peoples . . . it seems
very likely indeed that populations differ quantitatively in their
potentialities for particular kinds of achievement." [4]

I also asked the retiring president publicly whether he intended
to repudiate the published findings of Professor C. J. Connolly,
physical anthropologist at Catholic University, whose studies of
White and Negro brains disclosed, on the average, a greater sulcification of the frontal lobes in Whites than in Negroes.[5]

And I asked the retiring president whether he intended to
repudiate the published statement of Dr. Garrett Hardin, Professor
of Biology at the University of California at Santa Barbara, which
read as follows: "As a result of recent findings in the fields of
physiological genetics and population genetics, particularly as regards blood groups, the applicability of the inequality axiom is
rapidly becoming accepted." [6]

I then drew the attention of the retiring president to the fact
that none of these scientists were Southerners and I reminded him
that Professor Ruggles Gates, an Englishman who was at the
time probably the world's most experienced and distinguished
physical anthropologist and human geneticist, had made the public statement [7] that there were vast differences among races in
mental ability and capacity for development. I wanted to know
whether the retiring president had any *substantive* comment on
any of these statements.

At this point the retiring president had apparently had enough,

---

3. As used in this book, "equalitarian" means one who subscribes to the
dogma that for all practical purposes all races are innately (genetically)
equal in intelligence and character, and that the differences between them
are due chiefly to environment rather than to heredity.

4. *The American Anthropologist*, Dec. 1959, Vol. 61, No. 6.

5. C. J. Connolly, *External Morphology of the Primate Brain*, 1950,
Springfield, Ill. For the significance of sulcification (fissuration) as a measure of innate mental ability, see *infra*, p. 50.

6. *Science*, April 29, 1960.

7. In the introduction to Carleton Putnam, *Race and Reason: A Yankee
View*, 1961, Washington, D.C. Cited hereafter as *Race and Reason*.

because he referred my questions to the new president, a professor at the University of California at Berkeley, who wrote me a letter which I consider a classic. Confining his comments to the quotation from Professor Kluckhohn, he said:

"Relative to the statement by Dr. Kluckhohn, this in no way contradicts the position which was taken by the Fellows of the American Anthropological Association at the business meeting in Philadelphia. For example, people certainly differ in eye color. These differences are due to genetic causes. Very dark eyes are more efficient in the tropics, but this has nothing to do with the ability of people to participate in the democratic way of life."

To which I answered:

"My quotation from Kluckhohn was as follows: 'It seems very likely indeed that populations differ quantitatively in their *potentialities for particular kinds of achievement.*' [Emphasis mine.] You attempt to answer this quotation by citing differences in eye color and you make the obvious remark that these have nothing to do with the ability of people to participate in the democratic way of life. Kluckhohn spoke of differences in *potentialities for achievement* and these do have something to do with the democratic way of life. They particularly have something to do with the statement in your Philadelphia resolution which flatly equates White and Negro intelligence. Your answer is therefore completely beside the point . . ."

By now the new president of the American Anthropological Association appeared also to have had enough. At least I heard nothing more from him thereafter. Although I told the whole story in speeches and in television and radio interviews, no further comment was forthcoming from the Association or any of its officers.

I lingered over this episode because it was so typical of most of the attacks upon those scientists who offered the public unpopular but realistic facts on race. The Anglo-American scientific hierarchy, speaking through their various associations and magazines, invariably retorted with assertions, not with evidence.[8] The discouraging thing was how many people were taken in.[9] It

---

8. For further examples, see *infra*, Chap. II.
9. A Southern friend of mine with wide experience in press and public

seemed doubly disheartening to me personally in that, to the extent these retorts were intended to discredit *Race and Reason*, they were exactly the sort of thing which any objective reader should have been led to expect. In that book I had stressed the degree of political control over the life sciences, and the attacks now were direct proof of my point. They were transparent tactical moves by organizations which were the very mouthpieces of the hierarchy, depending solely for their persuasiveness upon their position as a hierarchy, and upon the force of numbers, never upon the facts.

The basic question here was a simple one: Were the American people to be given the evidence on innate racial capacities and variability, and then allowed to judge for themselves the soundness of the public policies which their legislatures and courts were adopting, or were they to be given only undocumented assertions which all the available evidence contradicted?

As I have said, the question seemed to me vital, not only in its bearing upon our domestic policies but upon our foreign affairs as well. The dissolution of the colonial system among backward peoples throughout the world, which the United States had done so much to encourage and which had produced such growing confusion and violence, stemmed from the assumption that these peoples had the innate capacity to maintain stable, free societies. The promiscuous granting of foreign aid, already raising grave problems, rested on the same assumption. So did proposed changes in our immigration laws. It was hard to think of any area of domestic or foreign policy which was not to some extent related to the

---

relations once remarked to me that Southerners did not believe the public really was deceived. "Any man," he said, "who thinks the average Negro is innately the intellectual equal of the average White man is too dumb to argue with." When I told him that polls taken in 1942 and again in 1956 by the National Opinion Research Center had shown, as of 1942, that 20% of White Southerners and 50% of White Northerners assumed equality, and that by 1956 80% of the Northerners and 60% of the Southerners held this opinion, he was incredulous. *Scientific American*, Dec. 1956, pp. 35-39. These polls combined Southern and Border states. Harris polls taken in 1963 and 1965 give later breakdowns, probably on a different allocation, but showing as of 1965 a 65% assumption of equality in the North. *Washington Post*, Oct. 18, 1965.

basic question, or where the truth was not essential to wise decisions.

To use charity, kindness, and brotherhood as justification for the deceit solved nothing. Concealing the truth was not charity, any more than lying to a patient about a cancer when an operation might save a life. Running away from reality was not kindness. Wrecking time-tested colonial systems of control among backward peoples and substituting systems which produced increasing misery and bloodshed were not acts of brotherhood.

On the other hand, presenting the facts about innate racial capacities to a legislature, government executive or court ought to result in a kinder policy toward school children, a better program for housing, a more successful attack on slums, a faster and sounder solution to unemployment, and a more constructive approach to the problems of the underdeveloped countries. This would not be a case of setting the clock back, but of turning the lights on.

Yet every day, on every side, government executives, judges, legislators, teachers and clergymen were acting in blind faith on a scientific hoax. More startling was the refusal of such men even to investigate the subject. Never once since the Supreme Court decision in 1954 had any President so much as invited for consultation at the White House a single scientist outside the equalitarian hierarchy.

As for the courts themselves, decision after decision based upon uncontradicted evidence had been handed down in the lower trial courts since 1954, had been reversed on appeal on grounds apart from the evidence, and had been refused review by the Supreme Court.[10] It was a case of a dogged defiance of reality, a plunging along in total darkness while riots raged, crime rose, and schools deteriorated.

Gazing at the embers of my fire seemed to offer no solution to this mystery, but the riddle plagued me. What prompted the vast majority of liberals and a large number—probably a majority—of conservatives to close their eyes to the underlying truth? The underlying truth was the strongest weapon the South had on the

---

10. See *infra*, Chapters IV-V.

race issue, yet the South refused to use it. The underlying truth
was the strongest weapon conservatives had on the general political front, yet they also shunned it. To expose liberal dishonesty as
regards the Negro was both a graphic and expedient way to ex-
plode all the fallacies based on the equalitarian ideology, yet conservatives concentrated instead on economic and constitutional
questions which, at a time of unprecedented prosperity, had comparatively little appeal to the man in the street.

In fact, few of the arguments of the conservatives had much
validity except in terms of the correct answer to the innate-equality
dogma. If all races were innately equal, then of course our social
organization, both nationally and on the world scene, was full of
flaws. If they were not, then the whole problem changed and conservative policies took on new meaning. Thus in refusing to challenge the dogma, conservatives were fencing on a scaffold while
liberals laughed as they watched the trap door open. It became
quite appropriate to refer to the conservative movement and the
Republican Party as the liberals' kept opposition. Their members
were condemned in advance, set up to be ridiculed and extin-
guished, amid the scorn and self-satisfaction of the left.

Nevertheless it seemed a fundamental tenet of most conservative groups, and certainly of the Republican Party, that the issue
was not to be raised. The very root of communism and socialism
which they so vociferously professed to oppose was thus to be left
untouched. It struck me as an incredible surrender, and the reasons for it demanded analysis.

Was there something somewhere in the Anglo-American social
climate which had destroyed the firmness of character and will, the
self-confidence and spiritual force, needed openly to face an issue
of this kind? Was there some relation between our contemporary
mood of appeasement and indulgence toward crime and juvenile
delinquency which accounted for our avoidance of the equality
issue as well?

Looking back upon my own youth before the first World War,
I surmised that there was. The mood of the times had changed.
Confidence in both the moral and physical force of rectitude had
gradually disappeared. Respect for distinction had gone, too—and

with it respect for authority in the home, in the community and in the state. All of these things tended to sap a man's courage to assert a vested pride in his personal heritage—might it not be just as true as to the heritage of his race?

Then there arose the argument that political expediency, indeed political necessity, compelled public men to avoid "hurting the feelings" of minority groups who might hold the balance of power in elections. But this, also, seemed an invalid approach. A balance of power position among minority groups could only exist if the White majority were divided, and the White majority would not be divided *on this issue* if it were properly instructed and courageously led. Some indication of what might be expected if the matter were considered by itself alone, even without leadership or instruction, was afforded by the 1964 referendum on the repeal of the Rumford Act in California. The vote was *against* open housing two to one, although President Johnson, an apostle of civil rights, carried California by 1,200,000 votes on the same day.

What folly it was for conservative leaders to suppose that cursing communism and dwelling upon its "conspiratorial aspects" as the John Birch Society did (all the while studiously avoiding any mention of race or the equalitarian dogma) could accomplish anything against the growing belief among Americans that the underlying tenets of communism might be sound! These Americans had been washed for decades in the powerful soaps of the equalitarian ideology—in the schools and colleges, in the theatres, on radio and television, in newspapers, books and magazines, and in the churches, until they were beginning to accept its validity without quite recognizing its kinship to communism or its indispensable connection with that movement.

In fact it was no exaggeration to say that to unmask the equalitarian dogma was to knock the bottom out of both communism and socialism. Neither could survive without it because both drew their major nourishment from supposedly unwarranted economic and social inequalities among men. To recognize that many of the inequalities were not unwarranted, that they were instead biologically constituted and consequently inevitable, was to cut to the root of every left-wing doctrine, called by whatever name. Simi-

larly, toying with the superstructure of these movements was
futile because every attack upon it could be met with counter-
attacks in the name of social justice. Indeed there was no possible
way of determining what social justice was until the equalitarian
dogma was dissected and exploded.

Social justice remained, of course, the goal which all men of
good will were bound to seek. It could certainly not be found in
mid-nineteenth century sweatshops nor child labor practices. Neither, on the other hand, could it be found in misleading courts and
legislatures on the variable capacity of races, nor in inflaming one
race against another by false preachments regarding the responsibility for unrealized hopes, falsely aroused.

With occasional but not statistically significant exceptions, in
America at least, a man might be poor and "underprivileged" for
one of three reasons: (1) because of innate limitations; (2) because of laziness and improvidence; or (3) because of social injustice. No one questioned the imperative to correct category 3.
But what the equalitarian did was to seek to blur the distinction
between all the categories and particularly to transpose 1 into 3.
This must increase rather than abate class and race conflict for
while most reasonable men would be willing to see their savings
and perhaps other fruits of their industry, intelligence and self-
denial taxed or destroyed to correct 3, few would submit indefinitely to such a procedure on behalf of 1 and 2.

Unless, perhaps, they were sufficiently misled. Then a different
situation developed. The question became one of how long a
society built on false premises could survive if the majority accepted the premises, and this in turn involved the importance of
the area in which the deceit was practiced.

Unfortunately in the racial area the importance was tremendous.
Could the barrage of excuses which came from the lips of liberals
explain away every decline is educational standards, every deterioration in morals, every increase in crime, every failure of foreign
policy? The equalitarian arsenal of excuses was almost unlimited.
Could it prevail indefinitely against the facts themselves?

And how long would our politically successful public leaders—
men like Johnson, Eisenhower, Rockefeller and the Kennedys, men

who had managed to ride the tide of consensus into positions of power as members of the "liberal establishment"—stomach their own blindness? The simple failure to investigate, to listen to any but members of the leftist scientific hierarchy, was startling enough in its revelation of wishful thinking. Second only to the heirarchy, and the managers of the mass media, such men bore the major responsibility for the continuance of the deceit. Was there no hope for a break in the ranks of these opportunists who bought their immediate success at the price of long-range failure?

One looked in vain for men in public life who understood the first duty of statesmanship as Theodore Roosevelt understood it. Roosevelt had written: "People always used to say of me that I was an astonishingly good politician because I divined what the people were going to think. This really was not an accurate way of stating the case. I did not 'divine' how the people were going to think; I simply made up my mind what they *ought* to think, and then did my best to get them to think it." Here was the difference between a public leader and a public panderer.

Surely there existed a wealth of wholesome and inspirational issues for the public man in the Anglo-American tradition. If other stocks could be encouraged in an emphasis upon their traditions and their achievements, if the Negro could be made the subject of a national mania, if all our minority groups could, in fact, be indulged in the practice of an intense racism, had not the time arrived for a little emphasis upon the values of the founding stocks which had built America in the most fundamental sense—given it its law, its language, its government, its religion, its pioneering enterprise and its stability of character? [11] Was it in the interests

---

11. The substocks of the Caucasian race which I call interchangeably English-speaking or Anglo-American were well defined by Theodore Roosevelt in 1881: "On the New England Coast the English blood was as pure as in any part of Britain; in New York and New Jersey it was mixed with that of the Dutch settlers—and the Dutch are by race nearer to the true old English of Alfred and Harold than are, for example, the thoroughly Anglicized Welsh of Cornwall. Otherwise, the infusion of new blood into the English race [more accurately, English amalgam] on this side of the Atlantic has been chiefly from three sources—German, Irish, and Norse; and these three sources represent the elemental parts of the

of those minorities who had either sought refuge here, or who had found a refuge by continuing here, that those values should be changed—and changed in a direction which must eventually produce the very conditions from which refuge had been sought?

The more one thought about it the less one saw any justification for the evasive, self-defeating attitude of conservatives, or the outright self-betrayal of Anglo-American liberals. One might attribute it to mawkish sentimentality, venality, blindness, or cowardice, but none of these seemed sufficient to account for the situation. Perhaps the element that appeared from my experience to come the closest to the root cause was ignorance, but a strange, self-perpetuating kind of ignorance bordering on hypnosis, an ignorance nourished by the pervasive power of the news and entertainment media after it had first been instilled by the academic hierarchy—an ignorance buttressed by feelings of guilt which the ignorance itself created.

Embers were no longer a match for a midnight in Maine. I decided the time had come for more wood on the fire before I rummaged further in the brief case which contained the all too short record of one man's effort against the obfuscation. A review of it might disclose whether there were points still worth making, or whether a digest of points already made might prove useful as a sequel to *Race and Reason*.

I knew of no way of combatting ignorance except with truth. St. Paul had said that the truth was mighty and must prevail. On the other hand I remembered a less optimistic writer who remarked that the truth would prevail only after no one any longer had any interest in suppressing it. Today it was staggering how

---

composite English stock in about the same proportions in which they were originally combined—mainly Teutonic, largely Celtic, and with a Scandinavian admixture. The descendant of the German becomes as much an Anglo-American as the descendant of the Strathclyde Celt has already become an Anglo-Briton . . . It must always be kept in mind that the Americans and the British are two substantially similar branches of the great English race, which both before and after their separation have assimilated, and made Englishmen of many other peoples. . . ." *Works of Theodore Roosevelt*, National Ed., 1926, New York, Vol. VI, p. 23.

many seemed to have such an interest. Only the inarticulate, nation-founding stocks in the United States—the divided and confused majority—had an opposite interest, and they failed to recognize it.

I gathered some logs from the woodpile outside, closed the door against the darkness, and spread a few more papers on the table under the lamp.

CHAPTER II

THE FANTASY

Which should come first—a deployment of the facts or a survey of the motivations and techniques which had led to their concealment? If one deployed the facts, and they were seen through the glasses of hypnosis, my experience led me to believe they would not be permitted to reach even the threshold of awareness. The contortions of liberal minds when confronted by the realities in this way had given me some bizarre moments.

Yet if one first examined the fantasy by exploring the sources of the hypnosis, one postponed dealing with the crux of the matter long enough to try the patience of the less bemused. It was a hard choice, but I came finally to the decision that it was best to begin with the hypnosis and to hope that the less bemused would bear with me for a chapter. There were enough other points in the fields of ethics and law which would require postponement to later chapters. In any case one must beg for some patience.

MOTIVATIONS

Without question I could state at the outset that modern anthropology as taught in Anglo-American schools and colleges is the *result* of a political ideology, not the source of it. The people who developed it, and their disciples who disseminated it, were almost all partisan and passionate crusaders for socialism.

They most certainly *wanted* all humanity to be innately equal, and they *wanted* to discover that the sole reason why inequalities existed was because of variable environments. Thus the responsibility for poverty and failure could be placed chiefly on society, not on the individual, and the rebuilding of the social order on socialist lines could be justified.

Another thing also was clear. Prior to the advent of Karl Marx in Germany and of Fabian socialism in England the infant science of anthropology had found no evidence of innate equality.

14

Before the middle of the nineteenth century Dr. J. C. Prichard, often regarded as the founder of this discipline, stated in his *Natural History of Man*:

"The organised world presents no contrast and resemblances more remarkable than those which we discover on comparing mankind with the inferior tribes. That creatures should exist so nearly approaching to each other in all the particulars of their physical structure, and yet differing so immeasurably in their endowments and capabilities, would be a fact hard to believe, if it were not manifest to our observation." [1]

Specifically as regards the Negro, the ninth edition of the *Encyclopedia Britannica* (1884) pointed out that "No full-blooded Negro has ever been distinguished as a man of science, a poet, or an artist, and the fundamental equality claimed for him by ignorant philanthropists is belied by the whole history of the race throughout the historic period." [2] Indeed, as late as 1921, it was still possible for Lothrop Stoddard (A.M., Ph.D., Harvard) to write the following passages about the Negro in a book issued by a leading New York publisher:

". . . in the negro, we are in the presence of a being differing profoundly not merely from the white man but also from those human types which we discovered in our surveys of the brown and yellow worlds. . . . The negro's political ineptitude, never rising above the tribal concept, kept black Africa a mosaic of peoples, warring savagely among themselves and widely addicted to cannibalism.

"Then, too, the native religions were usually sanguinary, demanding a prodigality of human sacrifices. The killings ordained by negro wizards and witch doctors sometimes attained unbelievable proportions. . . . Since the establishment of white political control . . . the white rulers fight filth and disease, stop tribal wars, and stamp out superstitious abominations.

". . . The white race displays sustained constructive power to an unrivalled degree, particularly in its Nordic branches; the brown and yellow peoples have contributed greatly to the civilization of

1. James Cowles Prichard, *The Natural History of Man*, 2nd Ed., 1845, London, p. 1.
2. *Encyclopedia Britannica*, 9th ed. (American Reprint), 1884, Vol. 17, p. 318.

the world and have profoundly influenced human progress. The negro, on the contrary, has contributed virtually nothing. Left to himself, he remained a savage, and in the past his only quickening has been where brown men have imposed their ideas and altered his blood. The originating powers of the European and the Asiatic are not in him."[3]

One could imagine what would happen today if a book with such passages were submitted to the same house for publication. Stoddard was one of the last to speak for pre-Marxian anthropology.

As would shortly appear, the change in attitude had no relation to any new scientific discoveries. Such investigations all reinforced the pre-Marxian view.[4] The new approach was due exclusively to "imaginative" thinking on the part of the passionate crusaders. As early as 1844, Marx himself believed, according to Sidney Hook, that "The primitives *actually* do not 'see' the same thing as the more developed races even though their biological structure may be the same. It is precisely because of *the different character of their social environment* [emphasis added] that they *see* differently."[5] Frederick Engels, Marx's colleague and collaborator in the major Marxist work on anthropological questions, continued and developed the emphasis upon environment and the attack on evolutionary concepts.[6] Concerning the motivation behind these men, one needed only to consider Marx's comment: "Labour cannot emancipate itself in the white skin where in the black it is branded."[7]

But it was with the arrival of Franz Boas that the story of cultural (environmental) anthropology, at least in the United States,

---

3. Lothrop Stoddard, *The Rising Tide of Color*, 1921, New York, pp. 90-92.

4. See *infra*, Chap. III; for example, it is now generally agreed among students of the problem, as the result of experiments with identical twins, that heredity outweighs environment (culture) in its influence on human beings by a ratio of about 3 to 1 on the average.

5. Sidney Hook, "Karl Marx and Max Stirner," *The Modern Monthly*, Oct. 1933, Vol. 7, No. 9, p. 554.

6. F. Engels, *The Origin of the Family, Private Property, and the State*, 1965, Moscow.

7. Karl Marx, *Capital*, 1947, New York, Vol. I, p. 287.

really began.[8] Because the man's background may in part have accounted for his point of view it seemed appropriate to mention briefly not only his early professional training but the social and political inclinations of his family. These threw considerable light on the formative influences of his youth.

Boas was born of Jewish parents in Minden, Germany, in 1858. Both his father and mother were radical socialists, and his uncle by marriage was Abraham Jacobi,[9] a physician who was imprisoned for armed violence in Cologne in the revolution of 1848. Jacobi later emigrated to the United States and was mentioned by Marx as active in promoting socialism here. Marx wrote, "Jacobi is making good business. The Yankees like his serious manner."[10]

Significantly Jacobi's second wife was Mary Corinna Putnam,[11] eldest daughter of George Palmer Putnam, the publisher, and when Jacobi finally died at the age of 89 it was at the home of a lifelong friend, Carl Schurz, formerly Senator from Missouri and Secretary of the Interior under Hayes. Thus a generation before Boas himself was to come to the United States a web of circumstances involving both Marx and Jacobi had preceded him— and had served to suggest the extent to which Marxist sympathizers had gained acceptance among intellectuals in America.

---

8. Initially, and before Boas' time, anthropology in the United States was the handmaiden of sociology, a science in which Lester Ward was considered the pioneer. Ward was an instructor at the Rand School of Social Science, operated by the American Socialist Society. Curiously enough, both he and his colleague E. A. Ross originally held the classical view of race. In 1905 Ross said, "The superiority of a race cannot be preserved without *pride of blood* and an uncompromising attitude towards the lower races." E. A. Ross, *Foundations of Sociology*, 1905, New York, p. 379. In 1938 he would be saying: "What makes . . . Congolese a mystery to us is not mental quirk but cultural background . . . Given our training, their minds would work as ours." E. A. Ross, *Principles of Sociology*, 1938, New York, p. 256.

9. Abram Kardiner and Edward Preble, *They Studied Man*, 1961, Cleveland, p. 135.

10. Marx-Engels, *Briefwechsel*, Dietz Verlag-Berlin, published under the direction of the Marx-Engels-Lenin Institute, Moscow, 1949, Vol. II p. 117.

11. For biographies of both Jacobi and Mary Putnam, see *American Dictionary of Biography*, 1932, New York, Vol. 9.

But to return to the young Boas, his education included no training in anthropology. His university degrees were in physical and cultural geography. His doctoral dissertation was in physics, the title of his paper being *Contributions to the Understanding of the Color of Water.* He made his first field trip, to study anthropological material in Baffin Land, in 1883 as a geographer for *The Berliner Tageblatt,* a liberal paper of the time.[12]

In 1886 he was a Docent in Geography at the University of Berlin. The following year he emigrated to New York and the year after that he served on the faculty of Clark University where the first Ph.D. in anthropology in the United Sttaes was taken under his supervision.[13] How he himself had achieved a doctorate in anthropology was not clear. He was a lecturer in psychology in 1896 and became a professor of anthropology at Columbia University in 1899, where he remained until his retirement in 1936. In 1942 he died suddenly during a luncheon, just after stressing the need to combat "racism" whenever and wherever possible.

Perhaps the most effective way to illustrate the trend of Boas' development was to examine two editions of his *The Mind of Primitive Man.*[14] In the 1911 edition he wrote: "Differences of structure must be accompanied by differences of function, physiological as well as psychological; and, as we found clear evidence of differences in structure between the races, so we must anticipate that the differences in mental characteristics will be found."

This crucial statement Boas omitted, without explanation, from the 1938 edition. One of Boas' students and followers, Otto Klineberg, suggested that "it seems highly probable that Boas changed his mind on this point."[15] To which Dr. George aptly replied, "Possibly so; but I know of nothing in the development of anatomy or physiology between 1911 and 1938, or since, to justify a change of mind . . .; quite the contrary."[16] Boas had said flatly,

---

12. So classified by the *Encyclopedia Britannica,* 11th ed., Vol. XIX, p. 579.

13. Kardiner and Preble, *op. cit.,* p. 137.

14. Franz Boas, *The Mind of Primitive Man,* 1911, New York; *ibid.,* Rev. Ed., 1938, New York.

15. Otto Klineberg, *Race and Psychology,* 1951, UNESCO, Paris.

16. Wesley C. George, *The Biology of the Race Problem,* National

"We found clear evidence of differences in structure between the races." One might now reasonably ask—what had happened to these differences?

While anyone's body could be modified by diet and exercise within the limits set by heredity, one could hardly take seriously Boas' personal effort in 1912 to show changes in fundamental structure through environment. In this case Boas went so far as to prepare a report for the Federal Immigration Commission which he called "Changes in Bodily Form of Descendants of Immigrants" and in which he tried to prove that head forms changed with the transfer of southern and eastern European stocks to American soil.

Henry Pratt Fairchild, a president of the American Sociological Society, commented upon this report in these words: "Two careful scholars, G. M. Morant and Otto Samson, have made an exhaustive study of the Boas report and related material, and their conclusions with respect to the Boas study are summarized as follows: 'In our opinion the data collected for the Immigration Commission are not capable of leading to definite proofs of these or alternative hypotheses of the same kind. . . . As far as the Jewish material is concerned, there seems to be no justification whatever for the statement, said to be "ample proved", that there is a "far-reaching change in the type [of immigrants]—a change which cannot be ascribed to selection or mixture, but which can only be explained as due directly to the influence of environment." . . . Our general conclusion is that considerably larger divergencies would have to be found in order to establish the theory that head-form, as estimated by the cephalic index, is modified directly by the environment.' " [17]

Fairchild added: "Boas apparently is expecting his reader to accept this one study as of sufficient weight to offset not only the

Putnam Letters Committee Reprint, 1962, New York, p. 81. Cited hereafter as George. Compare similar contradictory statements by E. A. Ross, *supra,* p. 17n. Persons who desire copies of Dr. George's work or other Putnam Letters Committee publications may now obtain them by addressing the Committee at Suite 904, 1730 K St., N.W., Washington, D.C. 20006.

17. Henry Pratt Fairchild, *Race and Nationality,* 1950, New York, p. 105. All of Chap. VII is recommended to the student of politically motivated scientific propaganda.

conclusions of dozens of able anthropologists, but also the commonplace observations of the layman in such cases, for example,
as the pure-blooded American Negro where there has been no
obvious modification of many basic traits after several generations of residence in the American environment." [18]

Nevertheless, as the years went on, Boas succeeded in becoming
the leading exponent of environmental anthropology in the United
States and in making this "cultural" or "social" form of the
science the most popular and the most publicized. He managed
to saturate both the public and his students at Columbia with books
and lectures on the dogma that environment is the dominant factor
in the molding of mankind, and to raise up a generation of disciples
who would carry forward his teachings in the next generation—
disciples whom Dr. George appropriately called a "cohesive
propaganda group".

One had no difficulty in understanding Boas in the context of
his time. Two distinct but converging streams of influence joined
to drive him. There was, first, his socialist philosophy, concerning
which it would suffice to quote his sympathetic biographer and
student Melville Herskovits: "In his political sympathies he
leaned towards a variety of socialism common among Nineteenth
Century liberals." [19] Indeed, Boas' family background had not
lain fallow. His record before the Special Committee on Un-
American Activities of the United States House of Representatives
showed 46 listings of communist-front connections. [20]

Secondly, Boas, popular as he was in several quarters, nevertheless could not escape the fact that as a Jew he remained a
member of an "out-group" in the America of his day. The endless
and bitter battle against "racism" which he and his associates never
ceased waging and in the throes of which he died, was apparent
in his work. He was obviously not without strong personal
incentives.

----

18. *Ibid.*, p. 104.
19. Melville Herskovits, *Franz Boas*, 1953, New York, p. 118.
20. Investigation of Un-American Propaganda Activities in the United
States: Special Committee on Un-American Activities, House of Representatives, 1944, *Appendix, Part IX.*

The same double drive could be attributed to a majority of his immediate disciples; for the others, the socialist influence sufficed. Even a cursory inspection of their names and connections suggested the nature of the forces acting on most of these individuals, and the impression could be fortified by a review of some of their activities. I was indebted to Dr. George for a tabulation:

Ruth Benedict, born New York 1887, died 1948; educated at Vassar and Columbia; lecturer in anthropology at Columbia, advancing to professor.

Isador Chein, born New York 1912; M.A. Columbia 1933; Ph.D. Columbia 1939. One of the Supreme Court authorities in the desegregation decision.

K. B. Clark, a Negro, born Panama 1914; Ph.D. Columbia 1940. One of the Supreme Court authorities in the desegregation decision.

Theodosius Dobzhansky, born in Russia 1900; graduate, University of Kiev; professor of zoology, Columbia 1940. Retired.

L. C. Dunn, born Buffalo, New York 1893; professor of Zoology, Columbia 1928. Retired.

Melville Herskovits, born Ohio 1895, died 1963; Ph.D. Columbia 1928; assistant professor (1927) advancing to professor of anthropology, Northwestern University.

Otto Klineberg, born Quebec 1899; Ph.D. Columbia 1927; research associate in anthropology, Columbia, 1929-31; psychology 1931; professor 1949.

Margaret Mead, born Philadelphia 1901; Ph.D. Columbia 1929; associate curator, American Museum of Natural History.

Ashley Montagu, born England 1905; came to United States 1927; Ph.D. Columbia 1936; Chairman, Department of Anthropology, Rutgers University 1949-1955. Retired.

Gene Weltfish, born in New York 1902; Ph.D. Columbia 1929; formerly lecturer in anthropology, Columbia.

This was the group of which Herskovits wrote: "The four decades of the tenure of his [Boas'] professorship at Columbia gave a continuity to his teaching that permitted him to develop students who eventually made up the greater part of the significant professional core of American anthropologists, and who came to man and direct most of the major departments of anthropology in the United States. In their turn, they trained the students who, with the increase in general interest in the subject and the recognition of the contribution it can make to human knowledge and human welfare, have continued in the tradition in which their teachers were trained . . ." [21]

The public had some familiarity with a majority of these names. Almost all the tracts on race distributed by UNESCO and similar organizations were authored by them, as were most of the books and articles available in bookstores and on newsstands.[22] Their views were often aired on network television and radio. But their personal backgrounds were not so well known.

Ruth Benedict, whose *Patterns of Culture* [23] sold over a million copies in paperback alone and was required reading in many college courses in the social sciences, began her studies at the New School for Social Research. This school was described by a *Joint Legislative Committee Investigating Seditious Activities in the Senate of the State of New York* as "established by men who belong to the ranks of near-Bolshevik intelligentsia." [24] Miss Benedict remarks that she "went to see Dr. [Alexander] Goldenweiser about taking a course with him during the first year of the New School for Social Research. I was an unemployed housewife with no knowledge of anthropology, and he took me on as a neophyte

---

21. Herskovits, *op. cit.*, p. 65.

22. On this point Dr. George comments: "At the University of North Carolina there is a course called Modern Civilization. This course is required of all freshmen and is prerequisite to other courses in History. Upon investigation, I found that one of the first required readings in the course is the integration tract by Otto Klineberg in *Columbia University Readings in Race, Personality, and Culture.* The library had on reserve three shelves full of the book to meet the calls of freshmen for this required reading. . . . Further investigation revealed that both at Columbia University and at the University of North Carolina, additional readings suggested are by people who have demonstrated a strong integration slant . . . It seems proper to ask, Why was no opposing point of view presented in these courses on so vital and controversial a subject?" George, p. 86.

23. Ruth Benedict, *Patterns of Culture*, 1959, New York.

24. *Revolutionary Radicalism: Its History, Purpose and Tactics, a Report of the Joint Legislative Committee Investigating Seditious Activities, filed April 24, 1920, in the Senate of the State of New York.* Part I, Revolutionary and Subversive Movements Abroad and at Home, Vol. I, New York, p. 1121.

. . . After a year of this work, he sent me to Dr. Boas and Dr. Lowie and suggested that I take work with them also." [25]

Margaret Mead stated that *Patterns of Culture,* whose preface she wrote (Boas wrote the introduction), went through eleven printings, was translated into fourteen languages and became "as timeless as the lives of the people on which it was based." Miss Benedict also co-authored with Gene Weltfish the pamphlet *Races of Mankind,* issued by the War Department to our military personnel during World War II. This publication was finally withdrawn because it was criticized as red propaganda. Later Gene Weltfish accused the United States of using germ warfare in Korea. Some of her other communist-front activities I had listed in *Race and Reason.* [26]

Melville Herskovits, too, attended the New School for Social Research and studied under Goldenweiser. [27] The motivation underlying Herskovits' career was suggested by a direct quotation from his work: "Let us suppose it could be shown that the Negro is a man with a past and a reputable past; that in time the concept could be spread that the civilizations of Africa, like those of Europe, have contributed to American culture as we know it today; and that this idea might eventually be taken over into the canons of general thought. Would this not, as a practical measure, tend to undermine the assumptions that bolster racial prejudice?" [28]

25. Sidney Hook, Ruth Benedict, Margaret Mead, "Alexander Goldenweiser: Three Tributes," *The Modern Quarterly—A Journal of Radical Opinion,* Summer 1940, Vol. XI, No. 6, p. 32.

26. *Race and Reason,* p. 18 n.

27. "Goldenweiser interested both Ruth Benedict and Melville Herskovits, who entered anthropology from the New School at the same period," Margaret Mead, *An Anthropologist at Work: Writings of Ruth Benedict,* 1959, Boston, p. 8.

28. Melville Herskovits, *The Myth of the Negro Past,* 1958, Boston, p. 30. A somewhat different view is taken by the French anthropologist Georges A. Heuse. In an article entitled "Race, Racismes, Antiracismes" in the Autumn 1965 issue of *Revue de Psychologie des Peuples,* Heuse remarks ". . . we can only hope that precious time will not be lost in recognizing the fallacy of equalitarian anti-racism. . . . In our effort to respect the full complexity of bio-physical and bio-sociological human phenomena, we often meet opposition from Jewish academicians who pose as champions of egalitarianism. . . . These champions, whose power and

There was nothing unnatural or improper about such an incentive in any member of a minority group. Whether it was conducive to an accurate evaluation of scientific evidence was a matter for the public to judge.

As for Ashley Montagu, his background served as a further illustration of this particular aspect of the problem. In addition to his career as head of the Department of Anthropology at Rutgers, Montagu acted as the rapporteur responsible for drafting the controversial Statement on Race for UNESCO in 1950. He wrote books with such titles as *Man's Most Dangerous Myth: The Fallacy of Race*. He had been anthropological advisor to NBC-TV, and had appeared repeatedly on such programs as David Susskind's "Open End", where the impact of his views was nation-wide. With his handsome presence and cultivated English accent he might well be regarded as the most effective popularizer of Boas on the national scene.

Yet Montagu felt impelled, after he immigrated to the United States in 1927, to change his name from Israel Ehrenberg to Montague Francis Ashley Montagu.[29] He also felt a compulsion to abbreviate his mother's name in his *Who's Who* biography from Mary Plotnick to Mary Plot.

Montagu's activities in the United States were interesting in other respects. In 1931 he taught at the New School for Social Research already mentioned. In 1942 he was a lecturer before the School for Democracy which was classified as communist by the New York Legislature and which merged to form the Jefferson School of Social Science, cited as communist by the Attorney General in 1947 and by the California Senate in 1948. In 1942 he stated that "Soviet Russia is the outstanding example of perfect management of ethnic group relations under unusually difficult

---

cleverness we admire, often believe that in denying race and racial psychology, they suppress at one and the same time both racism and anti-semitism. We are indeed surprised at their naive and erroneous belief."

29. U.S. District Court, Philadelphia, Sept. 25, 1940. Certificate No. 4931109. See also Marriage License Bureau, Borough of Manhattan, Certificate No. 22375, concerning marriage of Montagu to Helen M. Peakes on Sept. 18, 1931 at the Municipal Building, Manhattan, in which Montagu gives his mother's name as Plotnick.

economic conditions." [30] Since Russia has no Negro problem this statement seemed misleading.

During 1942 he was a sponsor of the Science Congress, conducted by the National Council of American-Soviet Friendship, cited as communists by the Attorney General in 1947 and 1948. In 1946 he sponsored the Independent Citizens Committee of the Arts, Sciences and Professions which merged subsequently to form the Progressive Citizens of America, cited as communist by the California Senate in 1947 and 1948. In 1947 he contributed to *Interne,* official organ of the Association of Internes and Medical Students, listed on page 34 of the Guide to Subversive Organizations. [31] In 1950 he signed a letter to President Truman from the American Committee for the Protection of the Foreign Born, cited as communist by the California Senate in 1947 and 1948 and by the Attorney General in 1948; and in 1950 he was a sponsor of the Mid-Century Conference for Peace, listed on page 50 of the Guide to Subversive Organizations.

If it were true as Montagu had stated that in his contacts with these various organizations he had been misled, then I had the impression that he was misled rather often, and that both in these connections and in his conscious or unconscious drives in the racial area he disclosed anything but a detached and scientific view.

Further examples seemed unnecessary. The converging streams of influence inherent in "out-group" resentments and the socialist ideology were extraordinarily powerful in combination, but were powerful enough singly. In fact, as the leftward movement of our times gathered momentum after 1933 and as the teachings of the original Boas group permeated the next generation, the Anglo-American elements in the cult became increasingly numerous. It was part of the pattern that they should be welcomed, and even recruited. They were of special value in lending an aura of impartiality to what would otherwise have been too obviously minority-group propaganda.

Thus slowly but surely, throughout and after the New Deal,

---

30. Ashley Montagu, *Man's Most Dangerous Myth: The Fallacy of Race,* 1942, New York, p. 82.

31. 87th Congress, 2nd Session, House Document 398.

motivation found fulfillment in the capture of a majority of teachers, of students and finally of the public. One must now turn to a consideration of the processes by which the hypnosis was achieved and maintained.

TECHNIQUES

Based upon my own experience I could state that there were four major methods involved, with numerous subsidiary variations. The foremost tool, from the standpoint of conditions as they existed in 1966, was the undocumented assertion by the scientific hierarchy channelled through the news media. Next in order were the two techniques of debate by avoidance and diversion—by shifting in the middle of a discussion from scientific to political grounds, a maneuver constantly executed by the hierarchy—and of argument by outright chicanery. Finally the whole procedure was secured by the suppression and persecution of scientists who offered to tell the truth. A few examples of each of these techniques would serve to illustrate a well-established design.

Nowhere perhaps had the technique of the undocumented assertion met with greater initial success than in the international arena through the United Nations. Here the no-race-differences dogma was flung like a banner high and wide in the form of the UNESCO Statement on Race, a manifesto drafted or revised among others by the Boas protégés Montagu, Dobzhansky, Dunn and Klineberg. The statement as first issued in 1950 read in part:

"Whatever classification the anthropologist makes of man, he never includes mental characteristics as part of those classifications. It is now generally recognized that intelligence tests do not in themselves enable us to differentiate safely between what is due to innate capacity and what is the result of environmental influences, training and education. Wherever it has been possible to make allowances for differences in environmental opportunities, the tests have shown essential similarity in mental characters among all human groups. In short, given similar degrees of cultural opportunity to realize their potentialities, the average achievement of the members of each ethnic group is about the same." [32]

This manifesto, by UNESCO's own account, was "extremely

---

32. *Race and Science: The Race Question in Modern Science*, 1961, New York, p. 498.

well received by the general public." [33] It was printed in a considerable number of newspapers in a score of countries and was frequently quoted in works dealing with the race problem; the Assembly of the French Union, at its meeting on November 20, 1951, adopted a proposal for the publicizing of the statement and its inclusion in school syllabuses.

But unfortunately for Montagu and his colleagues the Statement was in due course so widely repudiated by various biologists, geneticists and physical anthropologists that UNESCO was forced in 1951 to issue a modified but still unsatisfactory substitute. Some of the criticisms leading to the modification, and also of the modification itself, were printed in a booklet later published by UNESCO (without any publicity comparable to the original Statements) under the title "The Race Concept: Results of an Inquiry."

This booklet contained a critique of both the first and second Statements by Professors Darlington, Coon, R. A. Fisher, Eugen Fischer, Genna, Lenz, Saller, Scheidt, Weinert, Mather, Stern, Muller, Sturtevant and Snyder. Since it served to emphasize not only the undocumented nature of the original assertions, but their actual fallacy, it seemed proper to review a few of the complaints.

C. D. Darlington, Professor of Botany at Oxford University, England, wrote as follows:

". . . this Statement is partly untrue and capable of being contradicted at once. . . . Summing up, there is a danger that any statement about race issued by people who disagree with the Nazi views on race expressed 20 years ago by Hitler, Rosenberg and Streicher will be designed as a reply to those views. Since the Nazi views were emotional in expression and political in purpose, any discussion of them by scientists should be explicit, and explicitly separate from the expression of scientific opinions. Otherwise their opinions will be confused by the emotional and political issues.

"This confusion is found throughout the first UNESCO Statement on Race and in all the last six paragraphs of the second Statement.

"Today we understand very much more about how human

---

33. *Ibid.*, p. 494.

society has evolved than Darwin did; but few of us know the results of this evolution by our own observations better than he did. Fortunately genetics has given us every reason to agree with him. In *The Descent of Man* he writes: 'The races differ also in constitution, in acclimatization, and in liability to certain diseases. Their mental characteristics are likewise very distinct; chiefly as it would appear in their emotional, but partly in their intellectual, faculties.'

"By trying to prove that races do not differ in these respects we do no service to mankind. We conceal the greatest problem which confronts mankind, namely, how to use the diverse, the ineradicably diverse, gifts, talents, capacities of each race for the benefit of all races."

Sir Ronald Fisher, Professor of Genetics at Cambridge University, had one fundamental objection to the Statement which he felt destroyed the spirit of the whole document. He believed that human groups differ profoundly "in their innate capacity for intellectual and emotional development" and concluded that the "practical international problem is that of learning to share the resources of this planet amicably with persons of materially different nature," and that "this problem is being obscured by entirely well-intentioned efforts to minimize the real differences that exists."

Dr. Fisher remarked further:

"It appears to me unmistakable that gene differences which influence the growth or psychological development of an organism will ordinarily *pari passu* influence the congenital inclinations and capacities of the mind. In fact, I should say that, to vary conclusion (2) on page 5 [of the second Statement], 'Available scientific knowledge provides a firm basis for believing that the groups of mankind differ in their innate capacity for intellectual and emotional development,' seeing that such groups do differ undoubtedly in a very large number of their genes."

Professor Fritz Lenz, Professor Emeritus at the Institute for Menschlischer Erblehre, University of Gottigen, Germany, stated:

"Every attempt to restrict racial differences to physical differences is both arbitrary and scientifically unjustifiable. Linnaeus expressly included psychical differences in his diagnoses. Psychical hereditary differences are much more important than physical differences."

Dr. H. J. Muller, Professor of Zoology at Indiana University, United States, commented:

"Since there are very abundant *individual* genetic differences affecting psychological traits it would be extremely strange if there were not also differences in the frequencies of such genes, between one major race and another, in view of the fact that there are such pronounced differences in the frequencies of genes affecting physically and chemically expressed traits. That would surely be the attitude of the great majority of geneticists."

Dr. A. H. Sturtevant, Professor of Biology at the California Institute of Technology, wrote as follows:

"I have felt for some time that some of the arguments for racial equality were so obviously contrary to genetical experience as to be positively harmful—even when I approved of the conclusions drawn as to desirable social aims.

"There is excellent evidence for the existence of individual differences in mental characteristics—all the way from purely sensory differences such as color blindness to severe mental derangements such as phenylketonuria. On general grounds there can be little question that less easily analyzed genetic differences occur in all sorts of mental properties. There can also be little question that there are at least statistical differences between races in such genes."

As a final touch, anyone who took the trouble to look behind the facade would discover that the scientists who were asked to participate in formulating the UNESCO Statements were a selected group. Some of the world's greatest authorities in the field of race were not invited. These included Professor R. Ruggles Gates, Sir Arthur Keith, Professor Renato Biasutti, Professor Mario Canella, and Professor Bertil Lundman. Also omitted were American psychologists who had made original studies in this area, among them Professors Henry E. Garrett, and S. D. Porteus. In other words, the manifesto was a propaganda device of the most flagrant kind.

It might appear at first glance that as far as the UNESCO Statements were concerned the Boas cult had been sufficiently answered by the foregoing replies, but from the standpoint of the public nothing could be further from the truth. Here the alliance between the cult and the news media came into action and the "channelling" began. Newspapers, magazines, book publishing houses, and radio and television networks could all be counted on to disseminate the Statements indefinitely, and to see to it that the replies were forgotten. In fact, the media phase of the undocumented-assertion technique was so essential that it deserved special emphasis. I personally had repeated contact with it and could speak from first-hand observation.

I had already mentioned the resolution of the American Anthropological Association in Philadelphia in 1961. Although it seemed to me that the fallacy of that resolution had been sufficiently unmasked in public debate, it continued to be used by the media at every opportunity. It was even entombed in books attacking Dr. George and myself years after the event, with no mention whatever of the replies.[34]

When it came to answering undocumented assertions in magazines, the same result followed. For example, in the March 1964 issue of the *Atlantic Monthly,* Oscar Handlin, a Harvard professor and Pulitzer Prize winner in history, wrote a 5000 word article built around the sentence "There is no evidence of any inborn differences of temperament, personality, character or intelligence among races." Upon seeing it I wrote Edward Weeks, the editor, protesting the falsehood and asking for equal space to reply. Instead I was allowed a 300-word "letter to the editor", with rebuttal to Handlin but no sur-rebuttal to me.[35] This was typical of my experience with other magazines. A subject which required detailed treatment in depth was relegated, as far as the truth was concerned, to "Letters to the Editor" and answered by further undocumented resolutions and assertions to which no reply was allowed.

As to the newspapers, not too much difficulty arose in getting letters to the editor published as long as one avoided the issue of innate differences. Once the *New York Times* actually asked to

---

34. See, for example, James W. Silver, *Mississippi: The Closed Society,* 1964, New York, p. 27.

35. My request for sur-rebuttal under date of June 16, 1964, was not acknowledged.

publish a not-for-publication letter by me to the editor provided only that I would omit one paragraph referring to this issue. The reason, of course, was that while all other material regarding Negro differences could be attributed to White injustice, and the author made to seem a cruel "racist", the anatomical and genetic material could not. Therefore any attempt to put it before the public was forbidden.

Or almost forbidden. If one paid for an advertisement one could occasionally get it accepted in papers of secondary influence with strong, undocumented objection on the editorial page of the issue in which the advertisement appeared. But the papers of controlling influence would not even accept advertisements.

As an illustration, in the spring of 1964 the National Putnam Letters Committee [36] decided to offer, in full-page advertisement form, a letter I had written to President Johnson in which I carefully summarized and documented nine separate categories of evidence on the crucial question. This advertising procedure had been used in the case of my letter to President Eisenhower in 1958 with considerable success.[37]

Now, however, both the money and the advertisement were refused by *all* the papers which mattered most, in *all* the cities where it would have had the most influence, namely, New York, Washington, Boston, Philadelphia, Chicago and Los Angeles. The difference lay solely in the fact that the 1958 advertisement did not deal with the bed-rock issue—the 1964 advertisement did.

In the field of radio and television, my experience had been the same. Whenever the subject of innate race differences arose during any program the discussion leader would wait until the last minute and then, when no time was left to answer, would read the resolution of the American Anthropological Association as a coup de grace.

The most glaring episode of this kind developed not in connection with this resolution but with an occurrence which grew out of

---

36. The National Putnam Letters Committee was successor to the original Committee formed in Birmingham in 1958. See *Race and Reason*, p. 12.

37. See *Race and Reason*, pp. 12-14.

the annual meeting of the American Association of Physical
Anthropologists in the spring of 1962. Both the event and the
manner in which it was afterwards "channelled" by a television
network were so typical and so automatic that it seemed worth
reporting as one incident.

Moreover it involved no less a personage than the American
scientist Carleton S. Coon, at the time president of this Association. Dr. Coon, a New Englander by birth and background, had
received his A.B., *magna cum laude,* A.M., and Ph.D. from Harvard University. He had been awarded the Viking Medal in
Physical Anthropology in 1952. He was unquestionably one of the
most distinguished scholars on the world scene.

On the evening in question Dr. Coon was presiding at a final
session. Although several of the members had already gone home,
a resolution which had been discussed but tabled at a previous
session was reintroduced. This resolution condemned *Race and
Reason* because "there is nothing in science that justifies the
denial of opportunities or rights to any group by virtue of race."
No allegation was made as to what opportunities or rights, if any,
Race and Reason proposed be denied, nor by what authority
physical anthropologists, acting officially in that capacity, presumed to pass upon legal or political questions.

Before entertaining the resolution Coon asked for a show of
hands as to how many had read the book. Out of about seventy
in the room, three raised their hands. At this point Coon remarked
that under the circumstances he would rather resign the presidency
of the Association than preside further over the session. He then
left the rostrum and went home.

Confusion followed. I had not seen the minutes of the meeting
but it was a matter of record that no resolution reached the press
at the time. While one seems to have been passed, it was probably
felt that to release it under the circumstances would reveal too
much. Later in the summer, however, it appeared in a small New
England newspaper and was thereafter "in the open literature".

How "open" it was I discovered that autumn. On October 7,
during the Oxford, Mississippi, crisis, I received an invitation to
participate in an ABC coast-to-coast television program featuring

a general discussion of the race problem with Howard K. Smith as anchor man. During the course of the program the following dialogue occurred.[38]

Smith: "Sir, what do you think about this statement which was made by the American Anthropological Association? It says: 'The Association repudiates statements now appearing in the United States that Negroes are biologically and in innate mental ability inferior to Whites.' "

Putnam: "I might compare that statement with a recent book [39] written by the president of the American Association of Physical Anthropologists [Coon] in which he presents evidence, and takes the position, that the Negro race is 200,000 years behind the White race on the ladder of evolution."

Smith: "What are some of the findings?"

Putnam: "The findings are that there is from every standpoint —from the standpoint of zoology, from the standpoint of anatomy, from the standpoint of anthropology, from the standpoint of psychology—there is no question—the evidence is overwhelming in favor of a difference between the races in those elements which are involved in adaptability to our Western culture."

Smith: [In a changed background, facing the audience, Putnam cut from scene.] "Mr. Putnam suggested that Dr. Carleton Coon, the president of the Association of Physical Anthropologists, gave some support to his view. We asked that Association, and it gave us this statement: 'We condemn such writings as *Race and Reason.*'—that's Mr. Putnam's book—'There is nothing in science that justifies the denial of opportunities or rights to any group by virtue of race.' " [Interview terminated].

The legerdemain exercised here had to be seen and heard to be appreciated. By it, of course, the public was left with the idea that I had misrepresented the support given *Race and Reason* by Coon's book. I cited Coon in documentation of my thesis, and Smith arranged the interview to appear to refute the citation by quoting a resolution which had no relation to Coon's book and which Coon had done his best to oppose. Without actually making any false statement Smith had succeeded in leaving with the

---

38. The transcript is verbatim.
39. Carleton S. Coon, *The Origin of Races*, 1962, New York.

audience coast-to-coast a totally false impression of the facts.[40]

No better example could be asked of the smooth cooperation between the Boas cult and the news and entertainment media; it occurred constantly throughout the opinion-forming agencies of our society. And if one wondered at this close-bosom alliance, one did not have to seek far for an explanation. It lay once more in common motivations and mutual sympathies. Little perspicacity was required to discern that the identical drives which had swayed Boas were also within preponderant areas of the media, and that consequently the facilities for "channelling" were ready at hand. They operated twenty-four hours a day like clockwork. They made the technique of the undocumented hierarchic assertion as powerful as any.

Of almost equal importance one must rank the technique of argument by avoidance through political diversion or substitution. It consisted in retreating from one untenable scientific position to another, hoping to benefit from the ignorance of the opponent, failing which the shift was quickly made to non-scientific grounds such as civil rights and the Constitution.

I could think of many minor illustrations of this gambit. Before me on my desk was a *New York Times* review [41] of Dr. Coon's *The Origin of Races* by William W. Howells, Chairman of the Department of Anthropology at Harvard. In this review Howells remarked that Coon's book had been "pounced on with delight by the present cohort of racists"—by which he apparently had reference to such bigots as Dr. George—and then he proceeded to set up various specious scientific reasons [42] why George's interpretations of Coon were mistaken. Perhaps realizing how specious these reasons were, Howells ended with a sigh—half of triumph, half of relief. "Anyhow," he gasped, "I see no way of using such arguments [Dr. George's] to disprove the Constitution of the

40. I wrote a protest to James C. Hagerty, Vice President of ABC, on October 18, 1962, with copies to Nationwide Insurance Co., sponsor of the program, and Newton H. Minow, Chairman of the Federal Communications Commission. No reply was ever received from any of them.

41. Dec. 9, 1962.

42. I examined them in a speech before the Washington Putnam Letters Club on Feb. 12, 1963; see "These Are the Guilty," published by the National Putnam Letters Committee, *supra*, p. 14n.

United States." He planned this, I suppose, to be again the coup de grace, but it was certainly not science; it was, in fact, very bad law, as would soon be apparent.

Howell's retreat through the treacherous swamp of scientific fallacy to the imaginary rock of the Constitution was a pathway scientists tread often enough. But sometimes the hierarchy abandoned the preliminary retreat and took up their position on the rock from the start. In the November 1, 1963, issue of *Science* an article appeared mis-entitled "Science and the Race Problem," this time specifically attacking Dr. George and myself. The article was introduced as a report of a Committee of the American Association for the Advancement of Science (AAAS) and bore the signatures of what I presumed was intended to be an authoritative list of names.[a] In this article no attempt was made to answer any of the scientific arguments advanced by either Dr. George or me. The entire paper hinged on the point that we were "challenging the principle of human equality which is assured by the Constitution of the United States."

Since the matter occupied the pages of *Science* for several issues, and since it involved the whole validity of this type of technique, I might venture to offer my reply in part. In a letter published in *Science* and the *Congressional Record*,[a] I answered:

"It is totally incorrect to say that a 'principle of equality' is embodied in the Constitution. The 14th Amendment refers to 'equal protection of the laws,' but nowhere in this amendment,

---

43. A footnote to the article read as follows: "The members of the committee are Barry Commoner, Washington University, *chairman*; Robert B. Brode, University of California; T. C. Byerly; Ansley J. Coale, Princeton University; John T. Edsall, Harvard University; Lawrence K. Frank; Margaret Mead, American Museum of Natural History; Walter Orr Roberts, National Center for Atmospheric Research (ex officio AAAS Board representative); Dael Wolfle (ex officio). Responsibility for statements of fact and expressions of opinion contained in this report rests with the committee that prepared it. The AAAS Board of Directors, in accordance with Association policy and without passing judgment on the view expressed, has approved its publication as a contribution to the discussion of an important issue."

44. In *Science* on Dec. 13, 1963; in the *Congressional Record* on June 23, 1964, p. A3427.

nor anywhere else in our national charter, is there any support for a concept of social or biological equality. The principle which the AAAS committee dwells upon simply does not exist. . . .

"The committee errs also when it states that 'there is nowhere in the Supreme Court decision an appeal to science that relates to the nature and the origins of racial differences.' The finding of psychological injury to Negro children in *Brown*[45] is based upon evidence which has now been shown to have been misinterpreted by the chief witness in that case. The evidence actually proves that integration injures the Negro more than segregation. *Stell v. Savannah Board of Education,* 22 F. Supp. 667 (S.D. Ga. 1963).

"So the question immediately follows: Can this injury, which is due to an awareness of lower capacity, be overcome by contact with white children and the prolonged environment of white schools? And that answer in turn depends upon whether the Negro's limitations are environmentally or genetically conditioned.

"Public policy might conceivably justify the forced intrusion of Negroes into white schools, and the attendant turmoil, if the Negroes' limitations were due to environment and were temporary. By no possible argument can it be justified if these limitations are genetic and permanent. Hence, Dr. George's material goes to the very heart of the legal problem. . . .

"Altogether, 'Science and the Race Problem' is a tissue of fallacies and confusion put forward by men of no special qualification in the pertinent disciplines of anatomy and physical anthropology, who have acted with transparent political motivation. The timing with which the article was picked up and distorted by the general press denotes careful prearrangement on which I suppose the committee is to be congratulated."

The last sentence in this letter referred to the fact that, on the precise date of issue, stories regarding the article appeared to my knowledge in the leading New York, Washington and Chicago newspapers, followed by comments by columnists. Even the press of Australia remarked upon it.

Needless to say neither my answer nor those written by Drs. George and Garrett received any notice whatever in the media. The latter again served exclusively as a channel for the hierarchy, who this time were posing as scientists but acting in fact solely

---

45. *Brown vs. The Board of Education of Topeka,* the case in which the Supreme Court ordered the desegregation of schools. See *infra.,* Chap. IV.

as political commentators. They stood with all the trappings of their scientific authority flapping in the wind while they delivered themselves of declarations on law and politics about which they knew virtually nothing. [46] Meanwhile the public saw the authority and heard the declaration without realizing that the first had no relation to the second. The close liaison between the hierarchy and the media had achieved one more success.

On my table under the lamp I found another letter bearing upon the same point from a different angle. In the summer of 1964 there was held in Moscow, appropriately perhaps, a convention of 22 scientists called together by UNESCO. These scientists concluded their meeting by issuing the usual equalitarian statement on race, totally devoid of any supporting evidence. As usual, too, the press broadcast the statement with the customary references to how it "pulled the rug out from under" us bigots on the other side. [47]

But I happened to be personally acquainted with several of the scientists at the Moscow meeting and, whatever their political views, I knew the scientific views of some of them. I reached one of them on the long distance telephone, a man whose privacy I respected and whom I would not designate by either name or nationality. I asked this gentleman what had occurred to make him sign such a document and his reply, freely translated, ran somewhat as follows:

The Moscow meeting had been suffused with a sense of urgency. Something was going on behind the scenes "which made ruddy-cheeked men turn ashen." It became apparent that the cause was the explosion by China of an atomic bomb. The point immediately was made that now of all times China should be deprived of any propaganda argument against the West. Other

---

46. It was not that one objected to scientists expressing their political views. George and other truth-oriented scientists did this. One objected to the political views as a substitute for science and to the prostitution of the authority of scientific organizations by its use in support of political propaganda. George and his colleagues debated the scientific issues and took their political position upon the facts. The hierarchy did neither.

47. See, for example, the *New York Herald Tribune*, Oct. 2, 1964, p. 3.

Afro-Asian nations would be quick to listen, and consequently something must be done to remove from the West the "racist tag." There could be no better way than by signing the equalitarian declaration.

When I reminded this gentleman that such declarations undermined domestic tranquility in my country and betrayed those in the United States who were relying on the triumph of scientific truth, he replied that politically he feared the international situation more than our domestic problems.

After thinking this over for a day or two I sat down and wrote him a letter in which I pointed out that the sort of appeasement of which he had been guilty would not do a particle of good, that the more one appeased the more the encroachment was invited, that he would never win any help worth having by lying to, and fawning upon, backward peoples—all he would accomplish was the weakening of the United States.

Then I added: "There is a final point here about which I feel very strongly. If scientists wish to express their personal political views as private citizens, that is of course their privilege. But I do not think they have a right to get together as a group speaking as scientists (with all their public authority as scientists) and then falsify science in undocumented public pronouncements on political issues, simply because their private political opinions make them believe this is justified. They have no more right to do this than a group of doctors would have the right to join in a medical association and announce that a diet of spinach would prevent cancer, simply because as individuals they believe the sale of spinach would help the farmer."

On this occasion, of course, my telephone conversation and correspondence were necessarily private while the media saw to it that the UNESCO statement reached the man in the street around the world. More and more I could appreciate the validity of some remarks on the Nazis by Dr. Eugen Fischer, Professor Emeritus of Anthropology at the University of Freiburg in West Germany, a scholar who knew something about the subject at first hand. In one of the comments in reply to the 1950 Statement on Race by UNESCO, Dr. Fischer wrote:

"I recall the National Socialists' notorious attempts to establish certain doctrines as the only correct conclusions to be drawn from research on race, and their suppression of any contrary opinion; as well as the Soviet Government's similar claim on behalf of Lysenko's theory of heredity, and its condemnation of Mendel's teaching. The present Statement likewise puts forward certain scientific doctrines as the only correct ones, and quite obviously expects them to receive general endorsement as such.

"Without assuming any attitude towards the substance of the doctrines in the Statement, I am opposed to the principle of advancing them as doctrines. The experiences of the past have strengthened my conviction that freedom of scientific inquiry is imperilled when any scientific findings or opinions are elevated, by an authoritative body, into the position of doctrines."

Dr. Fischer here raised a point with many ramifications in the United States and Britain. No one witnessing the episodes already mentioned could doubt that freedom of scientific inquiry *was* being imperilled throughout our Anglo-American society. Nothing better suited both the hierarchy and the media. A major objective of their liaison, aside from the hypnosis of the public, was the suppression of truth-oriented scientists. In fact it deserved to be classified as a technique in itself, and again I had had some personal opportunity to observe it.

To begin with, of course, all the other techniques contributed to the weapon of persecution. They elevated the equalitarian dogma into a fetish by their ceaseless repetition through the media. The result was an academic climate highly unfavorable to free discussion, for it led to social ostracism, bitterness between colleagues, and personal disapproval of the individual worker and his family.

Beyond this the persecution technique raised higher barriers. With ruthless brutality it struck the pocketbook nerve. I remembered the case of a professor of my acquaintance at a Northern university who published a statistical study of the comparative mental-test scores of Negroes and Whites of similar socio-economic status. Since his findings were that the Negro averages were consistently and significantly lower, even under conditions of equalized environment, delegations from two racial pressure organizations—one Negro and one Jewish—requested his university to dismiss him, the doors of other universities were closed in his face, and a professional society in his field refused to admit him to membership on the grounds that his opinions might be offensive to its Negro members.

As another illustration I had on my table a letter from the president of a certain scientific society concerning a young member who voted in favor of a no-difference resolution at a meeting of that body. The letter read in part: "As for X————, he said nothing at all at the meeting but just sat there like many others; he apologized to me in advance for not voting on the [other] side on the grounds that should he do so his job would be in danger. He was probably right. I don't see what else he could have done under the circumstances."

Or I could quote from a letter from a professor of anthropology at a large Western university: "It is with regret that I must decline this opportunity to express again publicly my belief in his matter [of genetic race differences]. Letters, telephone calls, and threats after my statement in ———— were not favorable nor encouraging."

And I had before me a communication just recently received from a professor of biology at an Eastern university who had prepared material on genetic racial differences for publication: "Within the next few days [after my decision to publish had been reached] the President [of the University] summoned me to his office, and in the presence of the Dean of the Faculty and the Dean of the Faculty of Arts and Sciences, formally forbade me to publish any of this material. This was a formal and official prohibition, with some mumbling about academic freedom. I could only submit. There have been other pressures, most of which have been subtle. For example, my retirement will occur next ————, and from a more than adequate income, my monthly total will be less than ————. I will squeak through somehow, but I call attention to two federal and one state job which have died on the vine, and a hint from a competent source that I had better be quiet if I expect to get a book published [on another subject]." [48]

Henry Garrett summed the matter up in a note to me in 1962. Garrett had witnessed the technique as it spread from its source. He had received his M.A. at Columbia in 1921, his Ph.D. in 1923, and had then continued at the University [49] throughout the remaining years of Boas' life. "I knew Franz Boas personally," this letter read. "I was able to observe his influence as founder of the science of anthropology in America. . . . I was also able to observe the increasing degree of control exercised by the [Boas] cult over students and younger professors until fear of loss of jobs or status became common in the field of anthropology unless conformity to the racial equality dogma was maintained. . . . I can testify from repeated personal observation to the intimidation and to the pall of suppression which has fallen upon the academic world in the area of which I speak. It encompasses not only anthropology but certain related sciences."

In other words the economic sword swung viciously in hierarchy hands. The group was not content to see a federal government, already seduced by its dogma, use money to bribe state governments and buy their cooperation. It must reach down into the home and bank account of every truth-oriented life scientist in the Anglo-American world and break him if it could.

Finally I had to consider the technique of argument by chicanery. In view of the situation disclosed by the other techniques, perhaps this one should cause no surprise. Yet I marvelled at the intellectual superficiality of it, and mourned the ease with which the public succumbed.

I had already noted the type of irrelevancy contained in the reference of the president of the American Anthropological Asso-

---

48. For further examples see *Race and Reason*, p. 19.

49. For 16 years Dr. Garrett headed Columbia's Department of Psychology. He is Past President of The Eastern Psychological Association; the Psychometric Society; and the American Psychological Association. He is a Fellow, AAAS, and a former member of the National Research Council. He is a member of the editorial board of Psychometrika and, for 20 years, was general editor of The American Psychology Series.

ciation to eye-color,[50] and the sort of excuses offered by the
Chairman of the Department of Anthropology at Harvard in
regard to Coon's *Origin of Races*.[51] I now took from my table a
newspaper clipping reporting another attack on George's *Biology
of the Race Problem,* this time by Charles C. Perkins, Chairman
of the Department of Psychology at Emory University in Atlanta.
The clipping disclosed that in the course of this attack Dr. Perkins
had given the press the statement that "tests have proved that
Northern Negroes are smarter than Southern Whites."

When I first read this declaration I hardly knew whether to
laugh or cry. The fallacy in it had been exploded so often that
I almost thought Perkins must be joking. Here was the head of
an important department in a leading Southern university telling
a press conference something which the most elementary student
should have rejected as spurious.

The statement could easily be recognized as based upon an
analysis by Otto Klineberg of Alpha examinations given to World
War I soldiers. Klineberg had taken the four Southern states
where the White averages were *lowest* and compared them with
the four Northern states where the Negro averages were *highest.*
Here we had the familiar equalitarian trick of comparing the
best of one group with the worst of another and, of course, such
a procedure had no validity whatever. If an above-average Negro
were given a lot of advantages he would do better than a below-
average White man who had had very few. Wherever overlapping
statistical distributions existed, the top of one always exceeded
the bottom of the other. This was not the problem at issue.
The problem was what the average Negro would do when compared with the average White man under like conditions. The
evidence on the latter question left no room for doubt. [52]

The only mystery was why Perkins or Klineberg chose to
confuse the public mind with what I had come to call the

---

50. *Supra,* p. 5.
51. *Supra,* p. 34.
52. On the Alpha tests the average White score for the nation was 59,
that of the average Northern Negro 39 and that of the average Negro in the
best Northern state, Ohio, 49.5. The White score in Ohio was 67.

Klineberg twist. This struck me as the most blatant case imaginable of straining an argument to the point of absurdity in response to some conscious or unconscious compulsion. It would have been bad enough on the part of a layman. Coming from members of the scientific hierarchy, it was literally fantastic.

Then, taking another example at random, there was the case of one Donald C. Simmons, a member of the Department of Sociology and Anthropology at the University of Connecticut. In the January 5, 1963, issue of the *New Republic* Simmons launched his own attack on George's *Biology of the Race Problem* and its studies of intelligence in relation to brain weight by offering, in supposed refutation, a group of male Negro brains which he said were found to weigh more than a certain group of female White brains.

While slightly, very slightly, more sophisticated than the Klineberg twist, such a gambit from a member of the hierarchy must have left any person with even a superficial knowledge of the subject again nonplussed. Brain weight or size comparisons were never attempted without first allowing for sex and body size, and when these adjustments were made the averages were both consistent and clear. Could it be that Simmons did not know this? Or was the compulsion again so great as actually to preclude recognition that his argument had a probative value of zero? [53]

Even more startling had been my experience with the science editor of one of the nation's leading daily newspapers. This

---

53. It is hard to know whether to classify such cases under chicanery or under inexcusable ignorance. I am reminded of another case in which a member of the Wheaton College faculty studying for a Ph.D. in (cultural) anthropology wrote a book (James O. Buswell III, *Slavery, Segregation, and Scripture*, 1964, Grand Rapids) in which he devoted an entire chapter to an attack on *Race and Reason*, the burden of this chapter being that "culture . . . is so dominant a factor [in determining behavior] that for the comparative study of human society all other factors must be treated as if they finally cancelled out." How any modern preceptor in anthropology could write such a sentence in view of the 3 to 1 ratio of heredity over environment now generally accepted by geneticists (*infra*, p. 58), remains a mystery.

gentleman, whom I admired and valued as a personal friend, wrote me that informants whom he knew and in whom he had confidence assured him that "if racial differences exist they are so slight that they are submerged beneath the gross differences between individuals of any one race."

Here I immediately recognized the standard sop tossed by the hierarchy to the unwary among the press for re-circulation to the public. What seemed beyond belief was that it should have been offered to a man at the very top of his profession and that he should have been so easily deceived. To this editor I replied: "You are, indeed, correct that intra-racial differences exceed interracial differences. Intra-racial differences are enormous. If the differences in the averages between two races were as great as the gross differences between individuals at the extremes of the same race we would have on the one hand a race of imbeciles and on the other a race of geniuses. That sort of approach alone should be enough to alert you to the type of mentality you are dealing with, and the fact that people in your responsible position are willing to repeat it is a disquieting indication of the lack of consideration the matter has received." [54]

On its face, it ought to have been obvious that the argument offered this science editor had no bearing on the essential point. Here we had a difference "so slight" that it was "submerged beneath" something colossal. Carried to its logical conclusion it would mean that even if all Negroes were idiots and all White men Einsteins, race should remain irrelevant.

And these five examples only began the roster of trickery practiced by supposedly honorable men. In my daily routine I encountered chicanery, and a willing submission to chicanery, as a constant pattern. Taken together with the remaining techniques of the hierarchy, small wonder the hypnosis was complete and the fantasy rampant. Small wonder the man in the street was bemused.

Suddenly I was tired. I decided the hour had come to make

54. For results of a more thorough consideration, see *infra*, pp. 117-8.

myself a pot of coffee. In any case I had dwelt long enough on motives and methods. If I could present the situation plainly, then any sincere liberal who still believed that he was being told the truth about race by the educational establishment, by the mass media, or for that matter by politicians or churchmen, would have to be left to his dreaming.

For me, sleep of any kind was out of the question. The next folder in my brief case dealt with the scientific facts. That one I now pulled out and placed beside the others on the table.

CHAPTER III

THE FACTS

It would be wise at the beginning to set down the elementary statistics regarding the current performance of the Negro as a race in America. Although there could be no debate about these figures, and although the sole controversy raged over why they were what they were, nevertheless they remained in themselves an important introductory part of the evidential picture.

The American Negro on the average produced per capita eight times as many illegitimate children, [1] six times as many feeble-minded adults, nine times as many robberies, seven times as many rapes and ten times as many murders as the White man. [2] Conversely the Negro race produced one-sixth as many individuals with an Intelligence Quotient over 130, that is, in the gifted person category. [3] These were the undisputed facts concerning the performance and behavior of the Negro in the United States.

Overseas, in the only completely Negro republic in the Western Hemisphere, the Republic of Haiti, where the Negro had been on his own, so to speak, since 1844 one found the following situation from a self-government standpoint. After the Negroes massacred the last of the White population in 1804, Haiti remained a part of Santo Domingo until 1844 when it became a separate "republic." Between 1844 and 1915 only one Haitian President completed his term of office. Fourteen were ousted by armed uprisings, one was blown up, one was poisoned and another was hacked to pieces by a mob.

Between 1908 and 1915 the revolutions and assassinations

1. *The Negro Family: The Case for National Action*, 1965, Office of Policy Planning and Research, U.S. Department of Labor.
2. *Uniform Crime Reports*, 1963, Federal Bureau of Investigation.
3. Audrey Shuey, *The Testing of Negro Intelligence*, 2nd Ed., 1966, New York. Hereafter cited as Shuey.

increased so rapidly that a United States military occupation was needed to restore order. This lasted from 1915 to 1934. Thereafter followed twelve years of rule by a mulatto elite which ended in the resumption of control by the black military in 1946. Since then wholesale corruption and political murder have been the rule. [4]

Such was the more recent record of the Negro in the Western Hemisphere, and it could be duplicated on a descending scale throughout Africa. [5] The only question concerned the cause— was it faulty education and social deprivation, that is to say, environment, or was it something else? Environment was the exorcistic word, the abracadabra of the Negro movement. It was the catch-all excuse, heard from Zanzibar to Seattle, covering a period in time from the dawn of history to the present— although one might suppose, in the words of one writer, that in 6000 years the Negro's luck would have changed at least once.

Indeed it seemed to me it could reasonably be argued that with all due allowance for the environmental excuse, the Negro's current performance could stand, for the moment at least, as Exhibit A in my roster of *evidence* against the equalitarian. I emphasized the word, because the difference between evidence and proof was vital. The distinction was constantly neglected by equalitarians to confuse discussion. As one of their additional techniques of deceit it consisted in challenging isolated items of evidence as falling short of absolute proof, regardless of how

---

4. Liberals sometimes argue that other, non-Negro South American countries have similar records. The facts are that only Bolivia approaches Haiti in such indices as low life-expectancy, high illiteracy, low per capita consumption of newsprint, low per capita gross national product and low political stability, and all the Bolivian situation indicates is that neither the Negro nor some Andean Indian substocks of the Mongolian race are capable of maintaining stable, free societies. It does not qualify the Negro.

5. See *infra,* p. 61. It may also be noted that between 1945 and 1960, non-White immigrants to England numbered 1,000,000. This influx, mostly Jamaican Negroes, subsequently was curtailed by law. Although these 1,000,000 people constitute less than three per cent of England's population today, they are producing 75 per cent of the waifs now being received in British orphanages. Most are illegitimate and are Negroid in varying degree.

strong a circumstantial case the item made, and then deliberately avoiding an *assembly* of such items with its cumulative significance.

We would soon see that the weight of the evidence, the balance of probability, in every area of comparison between the White man and the Negro, favored the existence of innate differences in both intelligence and temperament. This was true whether one studied anatomy, histology, physical anthropology, kinesthetic maturation rates, electrophysiology, psychology or historical experience. In some of these areas the balance was less conclusive than in others, but in all it was on the side of innate differences, and the total taken together could not be called other than convincing.

Thus while world-wide performance admittedly did not provide absolute proof of the Negro's genetic limitations, it was certainly no evidence whatever in his favor. It was suggestive evidence against the equalitarian dogma. In this sense I could offer it as my introductory exhibit.

One came next to a more obviously probative item. In 1950 C. J. Connolly, Professor of Physical Anthropology at Catholic University, published certain findings in a book which Dr. James Papez of Cornell called "a reliable study of considerable scope the like of which has not appeared in recent times." The book was entitled *The External Morphology of the Primate Brain* and in part involved the study of 60 brains of Whites and Negroes.

The nature of Dr. Connolly's findings might be summarized in his own words:

"Comparing the two large groups of Whites and Negroes, while the variability is large and there is much overlapping, the mean values reveal significant differences. The dimensions correlate well with what we might expect from a knowledge of the cranium in the two races. The Negro brain is on the average relatively longer, narrower, and flatter than the brain of the Whites. The frontal region, as measured by the projectional distance to midpoint of central sulcus, is, relative to the total length of the brain, larger in male Whites than in Negroes, while the parietal is larger in Negroes than in Whites. . . . It can be said that the pattern of the frontal lobes in the White brains of our series is more regular, more uniform than in the Negro brain. . . . The White series is perhaps slightly more fissurated and there is more anastomosing of the sulci. . . . It is a matter of frequencies." [6]

The same conclusion had been reached many years earlier by Poynter and Keegan, who found that "the sulci and gyri of the Negro brain are undoubtedly less complex and easier of interpretation than those of the Caucasian." [7]

No evidence was brought forward, by the hierarchy or anyone else, to contradict these findings, although an abortive effort was made to evade their implications. Some critics argued that not enough was known about the function of the frontal lobes to evaluate the significance of the differences.

The reply here could be quick and decisive. The functional aspect of these lobes had been studied by Ward C. Halstead, bio-psychologist and Professor of Experimental Psychology, Department of Medicine, University of Chicago, who wrote: "The frontal lobes are the portion of the brain most essential to biological intelligence. They are the organs of civilization—the basis of man's hope for the future." [8]

Wilder Penfield, brain specialist and Professor of Neurology and Neuro-surgery at McGill University, considered at the very top of his profession, confirmed Dr. Halstead's position in these words: "The whole anterior frontal area on one or both sides may be removed without loss of consciousness. During the amputation the individual may continue to talk, unaware of the fact that he is being deprived of that area which most distinguishes his brain from that of the chimpanzee. After its removal, there

---

6. C. J. Connolly, *External Morphology of the Primate Brain*, 1950, Springfield, Ill., pp. 146, 203-4. Father Connolly, mindful of the equalitarian climate of his time and his position as a Catholic, is always guarded in his statements, which are full of qualifications. Thus he may easily be quoted out of context to an opposite effect from the general tenor of his book. He reminds us constantly of the existence of overlap. He raises the possibility that later discoveries or other samplings may provide different evidence. None has. For a further discussion of Connolly's problem, see my speech at Jackson, Miss., Oct. 26, 1961, *Congressional Record*, Jan. 25, 1962, Vol. 108, No. 10, pp. 830-831.

7. C. W. M. Poynter and J. J. Keegan, "A Study of the American Negro Brain," 1915, *Journal of Comparative Neurology*, Vol. 25, pp. 183-212.

8. Ward C. Halstead, *Brains and Intelligence*, 1947, Chicago, p. 149.

will be a defect, but he may well not appreciate it himself. The defect will be in his ability to plan and take initiative . . . although he may still be able to answer the questions of others as accurately as ever." [9]

Freeman and Watts reached somewhat the same conclusions: "It is not a question of intelligence in all this [consideration of the function of the frontal lobes], it is a question of the employment of intelligence. . . . Intelligence is not a function of the pre-frontal regions, nor is it altered by cleancut removal, except indirectly. . . . Something else in the personality is more important and presumably that something else is motivation." [10]

Not only did the size and the degree of sulcification (fissuration) of the frontal lobes imply certain specific capacities. They were in general a measure of evolutionary development. The frontal lobes of the rabbit were smooth. Connolly himself had noted "there is a degree of correlation between the sulcal pattern and the development status of the animal in the series of primate forms." [11]

The only other attempt at evasion I had heard in regard to Connolly's studies was a complaint that his sampling had been too small. The reply could again be pointed. If the hierarchy questioned the sampling, why had they never presented a better one? The hierarchy had the funds and the help of the great

---

9. Wilder Penfield and Theodore Rasmussen, *The Cerebral Cortex of Man*, 1957, New York, p. 226. Neither Halstead nor Penfield has made any studies of the relative characteristics of White and Negro brains and they are quoted here solely on the significance of the frontal lobes regardless of race. Both men have attacked George and me as "racists" while specifically conceding the accuracy of our quotations on the point in question. They had no evidence of their own to offer on the race issue, showed no curiosity about developing any, and confined themselves to criticizing the evidence of others as "inadequate." I examined this position in detail in *The Mankind Quarterly*, 1963, Vol. IV, No. 1, pp. 43-44.

10. W. Freeman and J. W. Watts, *Psychosurgery*, 1950, Springfield, Ill., p. 16.

11. Connolly, *op. cit.*, p. 360. It is of interest to note Brodmann's estimate that no less than 64 per cent of the total surface of the human cerebral hemisphere is hidden in the fissures as against 7 per cent in the lowest monkey. See Penfield and Rasmussen, *op. cit.*, p. 206.

foundations, the opposition did not. Was it possible that the hierarchy *feared* to conduct further studies? I left the question open, but I had no hesitation in classifying Connolly's material as Exhibit B, my second item of evidence.

Now for the third. In 1934 F. W. Vint of the Medical Research Laboratory, Kenya, Africa, published the results of a comparative study of Negro and European brains in which he found that the supragranular layer of the Negro cortex was about 15 per cent thinner than the Whites.[12] On the significance of this finding one could quote Dr. George: "Since structure is a guide to general functions in all those activities that have been adequately analyzed, it would seem rash to disregard structure in any consideration of the higher mental functions. In this connection it seems very significant to me that the cells of the infragranular layer have extensive primary connections with the lower brain centers while the connections of the cells of the supragranular layer are largely intracortical. This is powerful evidence of their primary participation in the special functions of the cortex—the organ of civilization."[13]

Thus the thickness of the supragranular layers, which increases as one moves up the scale from animals to man, could be said to be another measure of evolutionary development. The supragranular layers in the dog are one-half the thickness of those in the ape, and the thickness of the ape's only three-fourths the thickness in man.[14] In the case of the Negro their relative thinness again suggested his position on the evolutionary scale.

Vint went further. He both confirmed a significant simplicity in the convolutional pattern of the Negro and in addition discovered racial differences in the cyto-architecture of the frontal cortex—a paucity of large pyramidal neurons and an excess of small primitive cells in this area.[15]

---

12. F. W. Vint, "The Brain of the Kenya Native," 1934, *Journal of Anatomy*, Vol. 68, pp. 216-223.
13. Personal letter to the author. See *The Mankind Quarterly, op. cit.*, pp. 44-46.

To my knowledge, the only attempt yet made to discredit Vint's findings consisted in the suggestion that differences in health or preservative techniques between the European brains which were measured in Europe and the Negro brains which were measured in East Africa might have caused differences in shrinkage which would invalidate his findings. Dr. George replied that there was no reason to assume that such shrinkage would affect the Negro's supragranular layer without at the same time affecting his lamina zonalis, or the visuosensory area of his infragranular layer, which Vint had found to be *thicker* in the Negro than in the White.

Again any new studies by those who might wish to contradict Vint were notable by their absence. And so here we had Exhibit C.

Next one came to the subject of brain weight which Simmons had attempted to confuse. There could be no argument about the fact that, other things being equal (such as sex, body size, proportion of parts and sulcification), the weight of the brain correlated with intelligence. This was true throughout the series of vertebrate animals. A 300-400 pound alligator had a brain of about 15 grams—and little sense. A 300-400 pound porpoise had a brain weight around 1700 grams and was noted for its intelligence. [16]

Among human races numerous studies had been made of the comparative weights of White and Negro brains with results that all fell within the range of about an 8-12 per cent lower weight for the Negro brain. Such studies were published by Bean, Pearl, Vint, Tilney, Gordon, Todd and others. [17]

---

14. J. S. Bolton, *The Brain in Health and Disease*, 1914, London.

15. F. W. Vint, *op. cit.*; also R. Ruggles Gates, *Human Genetics*, 1946, New York, Vol. II, p. 1138.

16. George Crile, *Intelligence, Power and Personality*, 1941, New York.

17. Bennet Bean, 1906, *American Journal of Anatomy* 5:353-432; H. L. Gordon, "Amentia in the East African," 1934, *Eugenics Review*, 25:223-235. In addition to the difference in brain weight, Gordon notes that the East African native brain grows less after puberty than the European. Bright 14-year-old native boys fail to fulfill their promise. Starting at 10 years, the brain capacity starts less than the White and shows a flatter

I had never seen any findings which disputed these, although constant efforts like Simmons' occurred to confuse the issue by injecting variables which properly were eliminated in the initial hypothesis. The evidence was simply that, as a racial average, the Negro brain was lighter than the White and that this, in turn, indicated a lower average level of intelligence and evolutionary grade. [18] In the words of Dr. Coon, "among living populations—absolute brain size is generally, although not necessarily individually, related to achievement."[19]

In point of fact, in brain-weight comparisons one passed beyond a matter of simple evidence and approached the field of positive proof. But for the moment I was satisfied simply to classify the material as Exhibit D.

The preceding Exhibits from the sciences of anatomy and histology had recently gained support from physical anthropology. By the evidence of fossil remains in Europe and Africa, Dr. Coon's *Origin of Races* [20] had documented the hypothesis that the White race crossed the evolutionary threshold from *Homo erectus* to *Homo sapiens* some 200,000 years ahead of the Negro.

In this book Coon referred to the "great variability of twentieth-century human beings in *evolutionary grades* [emphasis mine] as well as in racial lines." He also said: "It is a fair inference that fossil men now extinct were less gifted than their descendants who have larger brains, that the subspecies which crossed the evolutionary threshold into the category of *Homo sapiens* the earliest have evolved the most and that the obvious

growth curve; Piersol's *Human Anatomy*, 9th Ed., 1936, Philadelphia, p. 1196. Piersol says: "Considered in relation to great groups, as to people or races, brain weight has been found to correspond to the general plane of intelligence and culture." Quantity is not the sole factor. Differences in the quality of nerve cells and of their organization may exist; Raymond Pearl, *Science*, 1934, 80:431-434; Frederick Tilney, *The Brain from Ape to Man*, 1928, New York; T. Wingate Todd, *American Journal of Physical Anthropology*, 6:97-194; F. W. Vint, *op. cit.*, pp. 216-223; Olaf Larsell, *Morris's Human Anatomy*, 10th Ed., 1942, Philadelphia, p. 901.

18. See generally, G. von Bonin, *The Evolution of the Human Brain*, 1963, Chicago.

19. "Race and Ecology in Man," 1959, *Cold Spring Harbor Symposia on Quantitative Biology*, Vol. 24, p. 156.   20. *Supra*, p. 33n.

correlation between the length of time a subspecies has been in
the *sapiens* state and the levels of civilization attained by some
of its populations may be related phenomena."

Coon pointed out that certain regions of the earth south
of the equator, among them Central and South Africa, were
areas of refuge during the Pleistocene and formed what might
be called stagnation points where evolution was notably retarded,
both in the development of man and other forms of life. "The
survival of *Homo erectus* in these antipodal Edens," Coon continued, "was not disturbed until no earlier than about 30,000
years ago, almost a quarter of a million years after the first
appearance of *Homo sapiens* in regions nearer the center of
evolutionary activity." [21]

No serious attempt was made to refute the hypothesis of
The Origin of Races, although a smoke screen of undocumented
general denials and prolix evasions of the issue appeared in the
journals. Theodosius Dobzhansky challenged the likelihood of
parallel evolution, only to be met in Coon's rebuttal by specific
examples of such evolution, by the probability of peripheral gene
flow and by other documentation.

Montagu, of course, had his well publicized innings and was
similarly answered. [22] We needed only to note that on October
25, 1963, the Literary Supplement of the London *Times* in a
special number devoted to the leading scientific books of 1963
referred to *The Origin of Races* as "a landmark in the development of the science [of physical anthropology]." Here, then,
was Exhibit E.

---

21. Carleton S. Coon, *The Story of Man,* 2nd Ed., 1962, New York, p.
35. *The Story of Man* provides for the layman a quicker survey of these
materials than *The Origin of Races.* See the former book, pp. 28-38, 60-62.

22. Scientific criticism of the *Origin of Races* (there was the usual irrelevant deluge of political criticism) fell into five general categories: (1)
Objections that a polytypic species could not evolve into a new polytypic
species while keeping the same subspecies. But even Dobzhansky, Coon's
best known critic in the field of genetics, admitted that on this point Coon
was correct. Dobzhansky, in fact, conceded the point in his *Mankind
Evolving* (1962, New Haven), published before *The Origin of Races.*
Ernst Mayr, the Harvard zoologist and author of *Animal Species and Evolution,* 1963, Cambridge, was in agreement with Coon; (2) Coon was

Again comparatively recently, methods had been developed for measuring the speed of kinesthetic learning from birth to the first years of life—learning, that is, which involved the transition from uterine to infant patterns of muscular reflex and control. This speed seemed to be inversely correlated with the ultimate complexity to be attained by the cerebral cortex, which supported the established observation that in all mammalian life full mental stature develops early in direct relation to cerebral simplicity. Thus, neonatal kinesthetic development is more rapid among gorillas than among chimpanzees, and much faster among chimpanzees than among human infants.

It was consequently logical to assume that differences in the rate of kinesthetic maturation between human races would have a bearing upon the complexity or evolutionary status of the structure of their brains. In 1956 Marcelle Geber made studies of normal infants in Kampala, Uganda, for the World Health Organization. She discovered that developmental milestones were reached several times more rapidly by Negro than by White infants. [23] To my knowledge there had been no attempt to disprove her findings. [24] And so Exhibit F.

A second new science which suggested a difference in evolutionary grade was the study of the electrophysiology of the brain. It investigated the living brain by analyzing its wave

widely quoted, among others by Dobzhansky, as claiming that mankind evolved five times from *Home erectus* into *Homo sapiens* through five separate mutations. Coon, however, made no such claim. He advanced the possibility of threshold crossing in the five subspecies through peripheral gene flow; (3) This raised the question, if peripheral gene flow was in part responsible for the eventual spread of the *sapiens* mutation to other subspecies, why did it take so long? To which Coon answered, because man alone has culture and culture imposes barriers to gene flow absent in other species; (4) There were a few claims that a parental species cannot breed with its filial species and produce fertile offspring. That this was untrue was clearly demonstrated by J. W. Crenshaw, Jr., in *Human Biology*, 1963, Vol. 35, No. 3; (5) Why exactly five subspecies? Because man is a large carniverous animal and needs a large living space for each subspecies. Five is the number of faunal regions inhabited by man at that time, and his range was the same as comparable animals. For a cross section of the debate see *Current Anthropology*, October 1963; also *Science*, Feb. 15, 1963, p. 638, and April 12, 1963, p. 208.

emissions, their cerebral location and the brain's electrical responses to various stimuli.

In 1953 a leading electro-encephalographist, A. C. Mundy-Castle, published a study of 66 Bantu-speaking African natives and 72 European Whites. He found five different categories of difference between the two groups, the most interesting, perhaps, being the lower response to flicker on the part of the Negroes. Flickers were created by high-speed electronic stroboscopes. These synchronized light stimuli were insistent and urgent enough so that a directing mechanism alerted the entire brain, and the response given was a measure both of cerebral complexity and stability.

Nathaniel Weyl pointed out that a null or impoverished response to flicker implied "a failure of the brain to develop, in the areas of imagination, visualization and power of conceptual thought, toward anything approaching maturity." [25] Mundy-Castle summed up his own conclusions as follows: "Our main impression was that they [the Africans] reacted in a far more simple way than did the European group." [26]

To move this evidence into the area of proof would require further testing and the isolation of possible environmental factors, but no one could question the suggestiveness of the results or fail to wonder why a well-financed hierarchy so carefully avoided the subject. I could regard it as Exhibit G.

One came now to the fields of genetics and psychology. Racial genetics dealt with the transmission of physical structure from

23. Marcelle Geber, *The Lancet*, June 15, 1957, Vol. 272, No. 6981, pp. 1216-19 and *Courrier*, Vol. 6, No. 1, pp. 17-29, UNESCO, Paris, Jan. 1956.

24. For an effort by a confused layman, indoctrinated by the hierarchy, see *infra, p.* 98. In answering a question from this layman I have gone into the subject more in detail than seemed appropriate here.

25. Nathaniel Weyl, *The Negro in American Civilization*, 1960, Washington, D.C., p. 152.

26. A. C. Mundy-Castle, B. L. McKiever and T. Prinsloo, *Electroencephalography and Clinical Neurophysiology*, 1953, Vol. V, p. 541. See also P. Gallais, J. Corriol, and J. Bert, *Medecine Tropicale*, 1949, Vol. 9, p. 693. Also P. Gallais, G. Mileto, J. Corriol, and J. Bert, *Medecine Tropicale*, 1951, Vol. II, pp. 128-146.

generation to generation among races. It explored also the extent to which the effect of physical structure might be modified by environment. Genetics alone was valueless in a study of the Negro problem unless one first had established the existence of anatomical and physiological differences. Thereafter it became of decisive importance.

Psychology, on the other hand, resembled the material in Exhibit A. The study of the *performance* of the mind was not directly probative of innate differences; it was open in varying degrees to the challenge of environmental influence, and of course lent itself readily to the equalitarian technique of chicanery. But as in Exihibt A, there was a broad suggestiveness about its findings, and certain data that seemed more than suggestive.

Turning first to genetics, no need existed now-a-days to prove the inheritance of racial structure. Races by definition were simply gene pools of distinguishable and distinctive physical characteristics whose anatomy, insofar as it involved the brain, produced corresponding mental differences. The same could be said of the whole nervous system and of the endocrine glands.[27] I had already considered the views of a number of geneticists on this point.[28]

What remained to make clear was the relative importance of inherited racial differences as against differences produced by differing environments. The equalitarian, and his prototype the social or cultural anthropologist of which Mead and Montagu were such good examples, argued that while inherited traits might have some bearing on behavior they were lost in the sea of cultural influences. This was the core of social anthropology— man had something no animals possessed, namely, culture, and through culture he offset inheritance almost completely. But social anthropologists never asked the question: To what extent had the culture first been created, and then sustained, by genetic traits?

---

27. Coon, *The Origin of Races*, *op. cit.*, pp. 115-116, and works there cited.

28. *Supra*, pp. 27-29.

Fortunately the answer was available in studies conducted with identical twins raised apart in radically different environments. Here the inheritance was the same—only the environment differed. The results had been published [29] and as usual remained uncontradicted by any scientific counter-facts. Although the effect varied somewhat with different traits, the over-all influence of heredity was found to exceed that of environment in a ratio of about 3 to 1. Certainly this had an important bearing on the Negro problem and deserved its place as Exhibit H.

The field of psychology had been fought over more than any other. Yet once one got past the barricade of the exceptional Negro, which had no relevance to the essential point, [30] all the evidence was again on one side. Audrey Shuey compiled the results of forty years of research in her book, *The Testing of Negro Intelligence,* [31] and Dr. Garrett summarized them as follows:

"1. The I.Q.'s of American Negroes are from 15 to 20 points, on the average, below those of American whites.

"2. Negro overlap of white median I.Q.'s ranges from 10 to 25 per cent—equality would require 50 per cent.

"3. About six times as many whites as Negroes fall in the 'gifted child' category.

"4. About six times as many Negroes as whites fall below 70 I.Q.—that is, in the feeble-minded group.

"5. Negro-white differences in mean test score occur in all types of mental tests, but the Negro lag is greatest in tests of an abstract nature—for example, problems involving reasoning,

---

29. H. H. Newman, F. N. Freeman and K. J. Holzinger, *Twins: A Study of Heredity and Environment*, 1937, Chicago. Also Sir Cyril Burt and Margaret Howard, "The Relative Influence of Heredity and Environment on Assessments of Intelligence," 1957, *The British Journal of Statistical Psychology*, Vol. 10, Part 2, pp. 99-104. Also Sir Cyril Burt, "The Inheritance of Mental Ability," 1958, *The American Psychologist*, Vol. XIII, No. 1, pp. 1-15. Also D. C. Rife, *Heredity and Human Nature*, 1959, New York. Also L. Erlenmeyer-Kimling and L. Jarvick, "Genetics and Intelligence: A Review," 1963, *Science*, Vol. 142, No. 3598, pp. 1477-8. For a short summary, see *The Mankind Quarterly*, 1964, Vol. 4, No. 4, pp. 197-204.

30. See *infra*, pp. 92-93.

31. *Supra*, p. 46n.

deduction, comprehension. These are the functions called for in education above the lowest levels.

"6. Differences between Negro and white children increase with chronological age, the gap in performance being largest at the high school and college levels.

"7. Large and significant differences in favor of whites appear even when socioeconomic factors have been equated."

To take a specific example, a research project [32] in 1963 among Florida Negroes, a project supported by the federal government and therefore scarcely chargeable to bias against the Negro, was compared by Dr. Garrett [33] with a test of White children run by Drs. Terman [34] and Merrill on a normative sample of the White child population across the country.

There were 1800 Negroes involved and 3000 Whites. Garrett did not hesitate to use the country-wide White figures against the Florida Negro figures in this case because tests taken in the Southeast among White children disclosed I.Q.'s as high or higher than the Terman figures. [35] Perhaps the improvement of education in all sections of the United States in the last quarter-century accounted for the difference (the Terman tests were made 1937), but in any case the comparison could not be held to be unfair to the Negro:

IQ Intervals	White	Negro	Rating	Ratio White to Negro
130+	4.45	.1	Very Superior	44 to 1
120-129	8.2	.3	Superior	27 to 1
110-119	18.1	.7	High Average	26 to 1
100-109	23.5	5.0	Average	4.7 to 1
90-99	23.0	14.0	Average	1.64 to 1
80-89	14.5	28.0	Low Average	.5 to 1
70-79	5.6	30.6	Borderline	.2 to 1
Below 70	2.6	21.1	Defective	.125 to 1
Average IQ	101.8	80.7		

32. W. A. Kennedy, V. van de Riet, and J. J. White, "A normative sample of intelligence and achievement of Negro elementary school children in the Southeastern United States," 1963, Society for Research in Child Development, Monograph No. 90, Vol. 28, No. 6. Research supported through the Cooperative Research Program of the Office of Education, U.S. Department of Health, Education and Welfare (C.R.P. 954).

33. *How Classroom Desegregation Will Work*, 1966, Richmond, p. 9.

34. L. M. Terman, deviser of the Stanford-Binet test used in both studies.

Regarding this table Dr. Garrett commented:

"1. The average IQ of the Negro children is 80.7. The average IQ of the White children is 101.8.

"2. Five per cent of the Negroes achieved IQ's *above* the average White child. Conversely, 89 per cent of the White children achieved IQ's above the average Negro child.

"3. In the High-Average and Superior groups are found 31 per cent of the White children, and 1.1 per cent of the Negro children.

"4. In the Average or Normal group are 46.5 per cent of the White children, and 19 per cent of the Negro children.

"5. The Borderline and Defective groups contain 8.2 per cent of the Whites, and 50.2 per cent of the Negroes.

"6. The average Negro pupil (whose IQ is 80.7) cannot go beyond a national-standard Seventh grade curriculum; for half the Negro group, the Fifth grade is the maximum.

"7. Only one per cent of the Negroes are intellectually equipped (110 IQ and above) to do acceptable college work."

No attempts any longer arose to dispute the facts disclosed by such studies. The equalitarian response consisted solely of the old environmentalist argument that the tests reflected a condition caused by White injustice.

Garrett the year before had had something to say on this aspect of the matter. At the Sepember 1961 meeting of the American Psychological Association, the Society for the Psychological Study of Social Issues had passed the monotonously typical, undocumented resolution declaring that the evidence developed over a quarter-century pointed overwhelmingly to the fact that differences between Whites and Negroes were not innate. It even went so far as to say that "no evidence exists that leads to the conclusion that such differences are innate." Garrett answered this resolution in the *American Psychologist* for May of 1962, by a statement relegated as usual to the

---

35. See, for example, the studies of Dr. R. T. Osborne of White Children in a Southeastern County, offered as "Intervenors' Exhibit I" in *Stell vs. the Savannah Board of Education*, 220 F. Supp. 667 (S. D. Ga. 1963), and there subject to cross-examination. Cited hereafter as *Stell Transcript*. The findings and opinion of the judge will be cited as *Stell Opinion*. Osborne found a mean White child I.Q. of 103. The Negro mean was 81.

Letters section. In it he pointed out that there had been exactly five cases in which efforts were made to equate as far as possible [36] Whites and Negroes for environment—that is, for socio-economic background—and in every one of these cases the results contradicted the resolution.

After covering the data [37] in some detail Garrett summarized it as follows: "Negro overlap of white norms when groups are matched for various educational and socio-economic factors does not increase markedly as compared with overlap in random samples. This is true for elementary, high school, and college groups. Instead of the evidence for diminished differences between Negroes and whites of comparable status being 'overwhelming' as the SPSSI statement asserts, it is, in fact, nonexistent."

To any student interested in the *balance* of the evidence in this admittedly complicated area, one could recommend a reading of Garrett's analysis. It was certainly Exhibit I.

Thus we arrived at the last of the categories of evidence— the area of historical experience. In a sense it was an extension backward of Exhibit A, a vista of perpetually deficient performance, but here the hierarchy had developed two contradictory themes of response.

On the one hand they argued that the Negro had been isolated by geographical barriers from contact with civilizing influences and that White groups so isolated did no better than the Negro. On the other they advanced claims that the Negro had created magnificent civilizations in Africa, hitherto lost to history but now being discovered as their ruins were unearthed. One had

---

36. It is, of course, impossible to equate completely White-Negro environment without turning the Negro into a White man, which begs the question. One comes as close as possible by taking Negroes from higher strata of their population than the strata from which the Whites are taken relative to *their* population.

37. Among the more interesting items special reference may be made to F. C. J. McGurk, *Comparison of the Performance of Negro and White High School Seniors on Cultural and Non-Cultural Psychological Test Questions,* 1951, Washington, D. C.

no difficulty in demonstrating that both these themes were specious.

As far as isolation was concerned, I could answer the hierarchy out of the mouth of one of their own star authorities in anthropology, A. L. Kroeber, who, in an unguarded moment, wrote: "All in all, Negro Africa lies open enough to the main Eurasian centers to have presumably experienced a slow cultural 'bombardment' that constantly mingled new traits with old, foreign with acclimated, and acclimated elements with those indigenously evolved. Through the centuries and millenia, everything got worked over until it took on the native local color." [88] Arab traders on the sea and Arab caravans overland were in touch with Africa south of the Sahara since ancient times, and more recently the period of European colonization occurred. [39] None of this lifted the Negro out of his primitive condition.

As for the collateral argument about isolated and equally backward White groups, no one denied that White men at various periods had lived in caves; no one claimed that civilization blossomed spontaneously from all races at any particular stage of their development. Little doubt remained that it first arose in the so-called "fertile crescent" of the Middle East and spread from there gradually to the rest of the now civilized world. The point was that the Caucasian and Mongolian races, whether or not they were living in caves, more often than not proved responsive tinder to the flame of civilization when brought in contact with it, whereas the Negro as a race literally *never* responded. This did not imply that Caucasians and Mongolians had always responded. Relict groups existed among both races. But in the case of the Negro the whole race except for the occasional individual had always been, and still was, relict.

Regarding the opposite and conflicting argument that the Negro *had* developed "magnificent" civilizations now lost, I had pointed out in *Race and Reason* that there had been no "mag-

---

38. A. L. Kroeber, *Anthropology,* new Ed. 1948, New York, p. 765.

39. See further *Race and Reason,* pp. 24-25, 42-45. Also and in more detail, Robert Gayre, "Ethnological Elements of Africa," 1965-6, *The Mankind Quarterly,* Vol. V, No. 4; Vol. VI, Nos. 1, 2 and 3.

nificent" Negro kingdoms in Africa in any civilized sense, that such barbaric cultures as existed were almost certainly intrusive, that the Moors and Ethiopians were not Negroes, and that the Nubian dynasty in Egypt was a period of retrogression. [40] However, in recent years efforts had been made by the hierarchy to glorify the ruins of Zimbabwe in Southern Rhodesia and to make these now appear to support the "magnificent" kingdoms claim. A word about them might therefore be justified.

One could see at a glance that the Zimbabwe ruins were large and brutal in their impact. They were essentially primitive. While the labor which originally built them was concededly Bantu, the hierarchy argued that the culture and leadership behind them were Negro as well. Such, for example, was the view of the author of the chapter on Zimbabwe in the publication *Vanished Civilizations of the Ancient World*,[41] priced at $28.50 and published in 1963. It was the sort of superficially impressive presentation which the hierarchy could afford to make, and needed to make, in lieu of facts.

The photographs were excellent—too excellent. All one needed to do was to compare any of the views of Zimbabwe with pictures of the Acropolis at Athens, and he no longer cared whether the complex was indigenous in either labor or inspiration. The contrast was enough. As Timbuktu produced no Thomas Aquinas, so Zimbabwe produced no Parthenon.

Those who still wished to carry on the intrusive vs. indigenous debate could note that in the rubble of Zimbabwe had been found porcelains of the Ming period. Since the Negro was never known to engage in maritime trade these porcelains appeared to students outside the hierarchy to have been brought in by a non-Negro ruling class.[42] The most recent survey of the subject, made by Dr. Robert Gayre, concluded that "there is absolutely no evidence at all that Zimbabwe and the other similar sites were built by the Bantu [Negroes], except as laborers." [43]

---

40. *Race and Reason*, pp. 42-45. See also *infra*, pp. 107-8.
41. *Vanished Civilizations of the Ancient World*, 1963, Edward Bacon, ed., pp. 34-54.
42. Herman and Georg Schreiber, *Vanished Cities*, 1957, pp. 191-223.

Thus it went throughout Negro Africa. Apparently equalitarian writers were so self-deluded they could not realize that their own photographs discredited everything they were trying to prove. Having failed elsewhere to uncover anything to substantiate their claim of equality, they now sought in historical ruins and relics evidence which, when presented, confirmed the opposite of their case. The facts from history were as Arnold Toynbee stated them: "It will be seen that when we classify mankind by colour the only one of the primary races, given by this classification, which has not made a creative contribution to any one of our twenty-one civilizations is the Black Race." "

Driven from their conflicting defenses of isolation and lost ruins, some equalitarians finally retreated to the excuse of climate and disease, to the argument that tropical maladies and the heat were enough to account for the Negro's condition. I knew of no *scientists* who advanced this argument, but it was frequently heard from laymen.

Here again one needed only to reply that, on the one hand, there were many parts of Africa where the climate was good

43. Robert Gayre, "Zimbabwe," 1965, *The Mankind Quarterly*, Vol. 5, No. 4, pp. 212-243. Any student disturbed by an apparent contradiction between the primitive nature of the ruins and the intrusive hypothesis should note Dr. Gayre's comment on this point (p. 231): "It has been argued that the stone building techniques used at Zimbabwe are too poor to have been the work of peoples advanced in technology such as were the Arabs. This cannot be accepted by anyone who has lived in isolation in an overwhelmingly 'native' community anywhere. No matter how you plan, argue, cajole and teach, the final product is a compromise well below your own normal standards, but something the 'native' would not have been able to achieve without all that effort on your part. Missionaries and planters in remote places—even in countries like India which are much more advanced than Africa in basic culture—tolerate standards of building, furnishing and other workmanship well below those of their own native background simply because this is the best a few Europeans in an overwhelmingly 'native' milieu can achieve. That was exactly the situation at Zimbabwe."

44. Arnold J. Toynbee, *A Study of History*, 4th impression, 1948, New York, Vol. I, p. 233. As for Toynbee's attempt, as a member of the British establishment, to evade the consequences of this statement, see *Race and Reason*, pp. 52-53.

and, on the other hand, other parts of the world which had produced great civilizations where the climate was bad. Moreover, for a hundred years the Negro had been free of both tropical diseases and the incubus of climate in the old ex-slave settlement at Chatham, Ontario. Yet his performance there on intelligence tests followed the standard pattern.[45] In fact tropical diseases no longer could be blamed for the Negro's relative performance in the Southern United States.

The truth of the matter was that whatever influence climate and disease may indeed have had upon the Negro over tens of thousands of years, the result had by now become innate through evolutionary processes. I could paraphrase Nathaniel Weyl and state that "the fundamental barrier is less the action of climate and disease on the living generation than its cumulative action, over an immense time span, in forming the race." [46]

So now in ten exhibits the evidence was in from current Negro performance, from anatomy, histology, physical anthropology, kinesthetics, electrophysiology, genetics, psychology and history. Not one of these areas showed any support for the dogma of innate equality. All of them pointed to inequality, to a difference in evolutionary grade. Some of the data could be attacked as insufficient to constitute absolute proof; other materials were scarcely open to this objection. Taken together, the total must be conclusive to any reasonable mind.

There were, of course, counter-arguments and sur-rebuttals concerning specific items that could be raised throughout the materials and I was prepared to deal with these in due course.[47] On the general situation only two points remained to be emphasized. One was the falsehood implied in the resolutions of the two anthropological associations and in the statements of individual

45. H. A. Tanser, *Kent County Negroes*, 1939, Chatham, Ontario, Canada.

46. Nathaniel Weyl, *The Negro in American Civilization*, 1960, Washington, D. C., p. 178. See also as to climate, *Race and Reason*, pp. 45-46. Also George, pp. 68-70.

47. *Infra*, Chap. VI.

members of the hierarchy. The other point was that in addition
to falsifying the facts as to the balance of the evidence, the hierarchy was doing everything possible to prevent any knowledge
concerning that evidence reaching the people. All the power of
the educational establishment, all the massive and saturating influences of a vast Negrophile news and entertainment media, all the
cunning of politicians, all the pleas of the churches, and all the
international tentacles of the United Nations were being ruthlessly employed to deceive both our youth and the general public.
Against such regiments of darkness could the truth prevail?

It was a sinister question to ask in the darkness and chill of a
night on Mt. Desert Island. Our cottage was very quiet now.
The doors were locked. Should I go on with such a problem at
so late an hour?

Figuratively speaking, the hour was late too. And I remembered the last recourse we had had, we who could not believe in
the victory of so monstrous a deception. In our Anglo-American
society honest men had always had their final vindication in the
courts. Surely, in spite of the action of the Supreme Court in
1954, this recourse must still be there. The deceit practiced upon
the Court in the desegregation cases was clear enough now—the
misrepresentation of the evidence proffered, and the omission of
all the decisive scientific material. Once this was placed on the
record in a new case, the tide must turn—so we had thought.

And then as I sat there memories of a court-room came surg-
ing back—memories of a May morning in a little Georgia town, the
walk along the quiet street to the courthouse, the attorneys for
the NAACP at the table for counsel, the stifled sobs of Constance
Motley as the heart of the issue was reached.

This folder in my brief case I could hardly touch without a
rising anger. Yet the story it contained, unbelievable as it was,
had to be told.

CHAPTER IV

THE DAY IN COURT

Actually the legal story began long before that morning in Georgia. It started, together with so much else, in the Boas web and the many-sided aberrations which it spawned. Some understanding of its relation to the law was an essential prelude to the final crisis.

Just as no one supposed before the Boas cult became influential that there was any question about innate race differences, so no one in those days suspected the existence of a Negro "right" to integration in our schools. Indeed the fact that such a right did *not* exist had been well established in the courts.[1] To the proverbial man in the street there seemed no more reason to think that two races as physically different as the White and Negro had a legal right to mixed schooling than there was to suppose men had a legal right to use rest rooms for women. Since nothing in the legal or social climate suggested such a right, the sponsors of the Negro movement,[2] in close alliance with the cult, set themselves the task of suggesting it. The legal department of the NAACP was the practical instrument, using the law journals as well as the courts as "educational forums for molding opinion."[3]

The first task was to discredit the biological facts, and for this no better vehicle could have been asked than the rising dogmas of a "sociology" rooted in the Boas fantasy. As one writer expressed it in 1945, "the trend of racial theory . . . has been away

---

1. *Plessy vs. Ferguson*, 163 U.S. 537 (1896). See also *Cumming vs. Board of Education*, 175 U.S. 528 (1899); *Berea College vs. Kentucky*, 211 U.S. 45 (1908); *Gong Lum vs. Rice*, 275 U.S. 78 (1927).

2. The Negro "movement," as distinguished from what is now so often called a "revolution," of course began much earlier. The NAACP had started its work in 1909.

3. Clement E. Vose, "NAACP Strategy in the Covenant Cases," 1955, *Western Reserve Law Review*, Vol. VI, p. 111.

from physical concepts and biological processes, through cultural analysis [the Boas technique], and into a sociological and social-psychological study of social interrelations." [4]

No effort was spared to indoctrinate the Supreme Court by a barrage of articles in law reviews and sociological journals based on this "trend". Chief Justice Charles Evans Hughes had once remarked that "in confronting any serious problem, a wide-awake and careful judge will at once look to see if the subject has been discussed or the authorities collated and analyzed, in a good law periodical," and the NAACP saw to it that the new seed was widely sown in such sources. [5]

Much of the preliminary work had been done prior to 1954. For example, in the Covenant Cases (1948) dealing with racial restrictions in real estate agreements, [6] certain of the lower courts had become so surfeited with environmental briefs by *amicus curiae* that in one instance a court of appeals remarked:

"We well recognize that vociferous minorities of our citizens, instigated by politicians, not statesmen, clamor for judicial denial of public rights under the guise of public welfare . . .; but, the courts ought to be and are ever mindful of that basic thought which underlies representative democracy, 'Give all power to the many and they will oppress the few, give all power to the few and they will oppress the many . . .' [A] reservoir of protection is to be found in our guaranty of constitutional rights, per example, the right to private contract; and in the hesitancy of the courts to be swayed by that which is seemingly popular for the moment, but which finds little or no sound reason or precedent, either in law or equity." [7]

Naturally the NAACP did not permit such language to dampen its zeal, and the pressure arranged and encouraged by it continued

---

4. E. B. Reuter, "Racial Theory," 1945, 50 *American Journal of Sociology*, p. 456.

5. For a full discussion of this strategy, with citations, see Vose, *op. cit.*, 101-145, especially the section "Flooding the Law Reviews," pp. 130-133.

6. *Shelly vs. Kraemer, McGhee vs. Sipes*, 334 U.S. 1; *Hurd vs. Hodge, Uricolo vs. Hodge*, 334 U.S. 24.

7. *Perkins vs. Trustees of Monroe Ave. Church*, 70 N.E. 2nd, 487, 492. (Ohio Appeals 1947).

unabated. At one point a poll was taken of organizations that planned to file *amicus curiae* briefs to the Supreme Court in the Covenant Cases and the following responded: the American Jewish Congress, American Jewish Committee, Protestant Council of New York City, Japanese American Citizens' League, Anti-Defamation League (Jewish), American Civil Liberties Union, Negro Elks, Congress of Industrial Organizations, Anti-Nazi League, Board of Home Missions of the Congregational Church, National Lawyers Guild, American Indian Association and the American Indian Council. Eventually a total of nineteen briefs were filed, and the Department of Justice had agreed to appear on the "open housing" side.

Meanwhile full-length articles were published in *The Annals, Yale Law Journal, University of Chicago Law Review, National Bar Journal, Architectural Forum, National Lawyers Guild Review, Journal of Land and Public Utility Economics,* and *Survey Graphic.*[8] Needless to say, the vast majority of both briefs and articles were saturated with the Boas dogma. Not one word unmasking the scientific fallacy beneath the whole façade could be found. Apparently the Whites as well as the Negroes were already bemused.

On May 3, 1948, a unanimous Supreme Court decided in favor of the Negroes. The opinion did not mention a single sociological article. But no one could deny that the work of the NAACP and its cluster of associated organizations had been decisive. The foundation for the desegregation cases had been laid. The ghost of Boas sat on the Supreme Court, put there by "vociferous minorities" with only the forces of ignorance and intellectual inertia[*] in opposition.

The manner in which the ghost now entered the classic *Brown*[10] decision desegregating the public schools was somewhat oblique. When John W. Davis, counsel for the South in that case and a for-

---

8. Vose, *op. cit.,* 132-3, gives titles and citations for these and other articles.

9. Ignorant and inert in the sense of totally unaware of the scientific facts and the history of their distortion.

10. *Brown vs. Board of Education of Topeka,* 347 U.S. 482 (1954).

mer Democratic candidate for the Presidency, learned that the
Supreme Court had based its decision at least in part on sociological material which had not been introduced in evidence, he was so
stunned it was said to have killed him.[11] Courts never rested decisions on materials which had not been offered in evidence at the
trial because, as to those materials, both sides had not had an
opportunity to be heard. The only exception to this rule were
facts of common knowledge, such, for example, as the fact that
the sun rises in the east. Then a court could take "judicial
notice" of those facts. Apparently the Supreme Court now felt
it could take judicial notice of Boas—in other words Boas had
achieved the status of the rising sun.

But only obliquely. In the Covenant Cases there had been no
reference at all to sociological articles. In the *Brown* case, *in a
footnote* to its opinion, the Supreme Court referred to various
sociological tracts and at the end of the note added, "see generally Myrdal, *An American Dilemma*." This reference, however
oblique, was an effective way of saying "see generally Boas and
his disciples" for Myrdal's *American Dilemma*[12] was Boas from
beginning to end.

For instance, a characteristic passage from Myrdal, a Swedish
socialist, read: "The last two or three decades have seen a veritable
revolution in scientific thought on the racial characteristics of the
Negro. . . . By inventing and applying ingenious specialized research methods, the popular race dogma [that races are not by
nature equal in their capacity for civilization] is being victoriously
pursued into every corner and effectively exposed as fallacious or
at least unsubstantiated. . . . It is now becoming difficult for even
popular writers to express other views than the ones of racial
equalitarianism and still retain intellectual respect."[13]

Neither John W. Davis, nor anyone else for the South, was
given the chance to answer such statements. Clearly enough,
Myrdal's arguments could have been exploded by any informed

---

11. A mutual friend to the author personally.
12. Gunnar Myrdal, *An American Dilemma, The Negro Problem and
Modern Democracy*, 1944, New York.
13. Myrdal, *op. cit.*, pp. 91-96.

cross-examination had he been called to the witness stand.[14] Not only could Myrdal have been answered by evidence which existed in 1954; as of 1963 he could be discredited completely. I had already considered the reply to such of his statements as "the social sciences in America . . . have gone through a conspicuous development, increasingly giving the preponderance to environment instead of to hereditary." Freeman, Holzinger, Erlenmeyer-Kimling, Jarvik, Burt, Howard, Gates and their colleagues would have something to say on that score.[15]

But there was another, more serious aspect to the *Brown* case. The Supreme Court reached its decision bathed in the ambiance of Boas but with specific reference to the testimony of the Negroes' chief witness, Kenneth B. Clark, himself a Negro. The Court in its opinion leaned heavily upon the damage suffered by Negro children from segregation, as Clark conceived it—a damage which the Court said might "affect their hearts and minds in a way unlikely ever to be undone."

These words from the Court were based on evidence Clark presented [16] which consisted of a series of tests done on Negro children with dolls. Clark had shown Negro and White dolls to Negro children in a segregated school and had asked them, first, "which doll do you prefer?" and next, "which doll looks like you?" There had been some pitiful moments when, after choosing a White doll as a preference, a child was asked the second question and burst into "uncontrollable tears." A staff member of the NAACP later publicly remarked that "on the surface at least, Thurgood's [referring to Clark's] black and white dolls won the case, not the historians." [17]

But Clark's summation of his evidence was not confined to pathos. He stated that ten (later in the testimony, nine) out of

---

14. See for example Myrdal's attempt to discredit brain weight as a racial factor, *op. cit.*, p. 91n, by references to Mall. Compare *Supra*, p. 52.

15. *Supra*, p. 58n.

16. In *Briggs vs. Elliott*, 98 F. Supp. 529 (E.D.S.C. 1951), one of the cases consolidated for argument before the Court that resulted in the *Brown* decision.

17. Speech by Alfred H. Kelly, *infra*, p. 73.

sixteen Negro children had picked the White doll as the one that "looked like you." From this he concluded that "these children . . . have been definitely harmed in the development of their personalities . . . My opinion is that a fundamental effect of segregation is basic confusion in the individuals and their concept about themselves, conflicting in their self images."

Clark then proceeded to tell the Supreme Court that he had made previous tests "consistent" with those he entered in the record. Whether intentional or not, this was the reverse of the fact. His previous tests were not only not "consistent", they actually contradicted his testimony before the Court.

They had been made on 134 Negro children in segregated schools in Arkansas and 119 Negro children in unsegregated nursery and public schools in Springfield, Mass. The black and white dolls had been presented and the same questions asked. Clark's own conclusions on the results had been that ". . . the southern children in segregated schools are less pronounced in their preference for the white doll, compared to the northern [unsegregated] children's definite preference for this doll. Although still in a minority, a higher percentage of southern children, compared to northern, prefer to play with the colored doll or think that it is a 'nice' doll." [18]

That is to say, Clark's previous research, done on a much larger number of Negro children, indicated that any personality damage which might be disclosed by his doll tests was not only not caused by segregation, it was actually *reduced* by it. Clark had put on a fantastic performance. In the measured words of a federal judge

---

18. Kenneth B. and Mamie Clark, "Racial Identification and Preference in Negro children," 1952, *Readings in Social Psychology,* Newcomb and Hartley, eds., New York. For a discussion of Clark's self-contradictions in his later attempts to explain his performance in *Brown,* see the Scientific Statement submitted by Dr. Ernest van den Haag, professor of Social Philosophy at New York University, to the Senate Judiciary Committee in connection with Senate Bill No. 1731 (Submitted Feb. 12, 1964.) See also, generally, Ross and van de Haag, *The Fabric of Society,* 1957, New York, pp. 163-66; Ernest van den Haag, "Social Science Testimony in the Desegregation Cases—a Reply to Professor Kenneth Clark," 1960, Villanova Law Review, Vol. 6, No. 1, pp. 69-79.

in a subsequent case, "I am forced to find that the principal evidence of injury relied on by the Supreme Court in *Brown* was unworthy of belief." [19]

Thus, apart from the general deception inherent in the propaganda of the Boas cult, the Court was subjected to specific deception from its chief witness on a specific and decisive point. It appeared that "segregation with the sanction of the law" in fact abated the sense of inferiority which the Court imagined it created, although nothing could, in the nature of things, change the limitations themselves—the fundamental point on which the Court had been deceived. [20]

The whole situation brought to mind the confession seven years later of Dr. Alfred H. Kelly, the NAACP staff member already quoted, who stressed the importance of the dolls but whose function had been to arrange evidence on the historical question of whether or not Congress intended the 14th Amendment to require the desegregation of schools in the District of Columbia. [21] Dr. Kelly, Professor of History at Wayne State University, spoke as follows in an address to the annual meeting of the American Historical Association on December 28, 1961: "The problem we faced was not the historian's discovery of the truth, the whole truth and nothing but the truth; the problem instead was the formulation of an adequate gloss on the fateful events of 1866 sufficient to convince the Court that we had something of a historical case. . . . It is not that we were engaged in formulating lies; there was nothing as crude and naive as that. But we were using facts, emphasizing facts, bearing down on facts, sliding off facts, quietly ignoring facts and above all interpreting facts in a way to do what [Thurgood] Marshall said we had to do—'get by those boys down

---

19. *Evers vs. Jackscon School District*, 232 Fed. Supp. 241 (S.C. Miss. 1964).

20. For a further discussion of the relationship of the scientific evidence to the Court's decision, see *infra*, pp. 141-2.

21. That Congress did *not* intend any such requirement in the District, and consequently did not intend it in the states, would seem sufficiently clear from the fact that it did not desegregate the District schools. As to the legality of the 14th Amendment itself, see *Race and Reason*, pp. 97-98.

there!' " ²² While this might be permitted to the average partisan in a law case, it was not precisely the attitude expected of a "scientist." Kenneth Clark, moreover, had attempted something more than a sliding off the facts in his own effort to "get by the boys".

Altogether the background of the *Brown* decision seemed so redolent of fallacy and deceit as to be entirely unacceptable in a nation dedicated to the honorable traditions of our Anglo-American jurisprudence. And to those of us connected with the National Putnam Letters Committee it appeared high time something was done about it.

Consequently we were gratified to learn in the spring of 1963 that the parents of certain White children in the Savannah-Chatham County region of Georgia were preparing to intervene in a court action involving the desegregation of their schools. The Negroes, represented by the NAACP, were the plaintiffs and were demanding desegregation, the Savannah-Chatham Board of Education were the defendants, and the White children were to appear as intervenors.

This case, to be called *Stell vs. the Savannah Board of Education,* ²³ seemed to offer an opportunity to correct the situation at last. Now it would be possible to expose the fallacies and supply the deficiencies in *Brown.* The proponents of the environmental sociology, the cultural anthropologists, the Montagus, the Klinebergs, and the Clarks could be cross-examined under oath on the witness stand. So could the Garretts and the Georges. Finally, adequate press coverage would permit a beginning in the education of the public about the facts.

Therefore, on May 8, 1963, the day before the start of the trial, all of us who were interested in the White children's side,

---

22. Later in this speech the following curious passage occurs: "A good Freudian psychologist, I know, will be hugging himself with sardonic joy at this point, observing with self-satisfied glee that academic man obviously has as great a capacity for manipulating reality by myth in order to preserve his personal integrity [sic] as has any ordinary day laborer—perhaps an even greater capacity because of his superior myth-making abilities. I do not know." One wonders what Kelly's definition of personal integrity is.

23. 220 Fed. Supp. 667 (S.D. Ga. 1963). Cited hereafter as *Stell.*

and in the larger issues involved, proceeded to Brunswick, Georgia, [24] with high hopes. Carter Pittman, George Leonard, Charles Bloch and Walter Cowart were the attorneys for these children and established themselves at a motel where they were joined by Drs. Garrett, George, Osborne, Armstrong and van den Haag as scientific witnesses. It had been decided that it would be best not to embarrass Dr. Coon by asking him to enter the controversy; his position as dean of the world's physical anthropologists deserved detachment, but material from *The Origin of Races* would be sponsored by Dr. George and therefore subject to cross-examination by the Negroes. I joined the group on the afternoon of the 8th as an observer.

Attorneys for the Negroes were at another hotel, but we were advised that they would include both Jack Greenberg and Constance Motley, a mulatto, each of whom had played a part as counsel for the NAACP in *Brown.* [25] We did not know as yet that they would have no scientific witnesses. Had I suspected this, I might have felt some preliminary apprehension. I might have wondered if it could be possible that, having succeeded in shutting out all the vital evidence in *Brown,* the Negroes expected to keep it shut out now. Such a policy would require a surpassing confidence in the partisanship of the Supreme Court and of the trial and appellate judges. It would have to assume that ways could be found to avoid reopening a previous decision reached on the basis of deception and concealment when the deception was unmasked and the truth revealed. It would also involve a confession on the part of the Negroes that cross-examination of the hierarchy under oath was something they dared not face. Fortunately for our rest that night, none of us foresaw the future.

May 9th dawned clear and warm—a pleasant, early-summer day in the Sea Island country. The public benches in the courtroom were occupied early by both Whites and Negroes but the

---

24. The first two days of the trial, May 9 and 10, were held at Brunswick, the third day, May 13, at Savannah.

25. Greenberg had now become General Counsel for the NAACP Legal Defense Fund. He did not appear at the trial.

press was scantily represented. I did not remember seeing any correspondent for the *New York Times*. The swearing-in was soon over, and the morning spent in the examination and cross-examination of the Superintendent of Schools regarding the fact of segregation in Savannah-Chatham County and the problems that would arise if desegregation occurred. Not until mid-afternoon did attorneys for the White children open their case with the calling of Dr. R. T. Osborne as their first scientific witness.

Dr. Osborne, Professor of Psychology and Director of the Student Guidance Center at the University of Georgia, established his qualifications as an expert in the field of educational testing and personality measurement. Then he proceeded to disclose the results of studies he had made for the Superintendent in Chatham County:

Q. [By Mr. Leonard] "What conclusions did you come to in this study?"

A. "At all levels in the educational program there are differences in achievement between the white and negro pupils. The differences are noticeable at the pre-school level and persist throughout the entire program in the Chatham County Schools through the 12th grade."

Q. "Are the differences of a particular type only or do they vary in patterns or according to schools?"

A. "The differences are found in reading, achievement, mathematics, mental maturity." [26]

On cross-examination Mrs. Motley, for the NAACP, confined herself to raising the usual point as to the existence of overlap, which Dr. Osborne did not deny. Mrs. Motley then suggested that since there was overlap "these differences you are talking about don't have anything to do with race," to which Osborne may be forgiven for answering, "I don't understand the question."

Q. [By Mrs. Motley] "It [the difference] may be the result of the inferior education in the Negro schools or the Negro environment, right.

---

26. For a full discussion of these tests, including graphs, see "Intervenors' Exhibit 1" to *Transcript of Proceedings, Stell.*

A. "Either one. That's right."

Q. "Then it can't be attributed wholly to race, by your study, right?"

A. "Not wholly to race."

All this was a somewhat elementary mixture of the fact of overlap and the relative influence of heredity and environment which did not affect the point on which Osborne's evidence bore, and Osborne shortly thereafter was excused.

Counsel for the White children next placed Dr. Garrett on the stand but before he could do more than qualify himself Mrs. Motley confronted the Court with a threat intended to cut off further evidence. This was the tactic we might have expected— the move to shut out the scientific facts at the source, to prevent their even getting into the trial record, or reaching the public, whatever else might happen later.

Mrs. Motley: "Here we go, your Honor. We are going over the same thing."

The Court: "I will make the same ruling I did on the others. I am going to hear all of this evidence and you can make your objections when we get through with the evidence and then I will hear both sides. . . ."

Mrs. Motley: "Your Honor, I think that what the plaintiffs [Negroes] are going to have to do is to go to the Fifth Circuit, or some other court, and get a Writ of Prohibition, or something, against this kind of testimony."

The Court: "I have already ruled on that. I said that I was going to hear the testimony, and then after I hear it, then you raise your objections. . . ."

Mrs. Motley: "It is delaying an adjudication of this case, your Honor."

The Court: "The adjudication of the case will be delivered promptly, I will assure you of that, because Judge Tuttle [presiding judge of the Fifth Circuit] has ordered me to file it by Monday, but if I can't file it by Monday I am sure he will understand that I am still in the trial of the case."

Mrs. Motley: "Well, he has already ruled, your Honor, that this kind of testimony is not going to be considered in any court. He has tried to make that plain."

The Court: "Well, he is just one Judge, you know."

Mrs. Motley: "Well, I am as sure as I am standing here that the United States Supreme Court, after three times ruling that segregation is unconstituional, is not now going to reverse itself on this man's testimony or any other testimony."

The Court: "Well, let's don't bring it up any more. I have determined that I am going to hear this evidence, and after the evidence is concluded if you want to raise an objection at that time I will hear from you, but I have determined that I am going to hear this evidence. I have stated that three or four times. I am going to hear it. I think it is material."

Mrs. Motley: "Then we would like to make this motion———"

The Court: "———All right."

Mrs. Motley: "The Rules provide, the statute provides that we can take an appeal by a certificate from this Court to the Court of Appeals as to whether this kind of evidence is admissible."

The Court: "No, I am not going to do that. You can take it up in the regular course, if I decide against you. I have not decided against you yet, but if I decide against you, why, you can take it by the regular course, but I am not going to certify to the Court of Appeals of anything."

Mrs. Motley: "Well, the point is we want this question determined before all of this evidence is put into the record."

The Court: "Well, you seem hard to convince, but I am trying to convince you that I am going to hear it, and that's that. So, you may proceed. I don't mean to be discourteous but I said that to start with, that I was going to hear it all. This is an important case. It is a novel case. All right, you may proceed."

Of course, it was plain enough that the one thing Motley dreaded, and what she was beginning to realize might be coming, was a real examination of all the evidence so long evaded and suppressed. It was an understandable fear, disclosed under mounting tension. She subsided for the moment but later in the course of Dr. Garrett's testimony this exchange occurred:

Mrs. Motley: "Well, your Honor, I would like to say this then: Judge Tuttle has said that we can renew our motion on Monday for the appointment of another Judge to hear this case, and on Monday we plan to do that. We don't plan to appear in Savannah on Monday. We plan to file that motion in the Fifth Circuit."

The Court: "That's your privilege. However, I think that is more or less a threat, and let the record show that, but that isn't bothering me a bit. I am going to do what I think is right, and I am sure Judge Tuttle will agree with me that is right."

A statement by the Court later in the proceedings disclosed that Mrs. Motley did apply and was refused. [27] The Fifth Circuit was not prepared to go quite so far so soon.

But to return to the testimony of Dr. Garrett, he proceeded to present on a national scale evidence of the same nature as that offered by Dr. Osborne on a local scale, with special emphasis on those tests which had revealed no appreciable improvement in Negro performance when socio-economic factors were equated. The obvious implication that this made the causes of the difference in performance primarily genetic was again not lost on Mrs. Motley:

Q. [By Mrs. Motley] "Now, why is there such a tremendous difference between the overlap in other parts of the country and Chatham County?"

A. "Well, I can only hazard a guess at that. I think the southern Negro is mostly rural or agricultural. He is not very selective. The selective ones probably have gone north. He is unmixed, generally, and I think a lot of those factors come in."

Q. "So, it doesn't have to do with race, necessarily, does it, just environment?"

A. "I think it has to do with environment. It has to do with race, too."

Q. "Well, what does [intelligence] quotient have to do with race?"

A. "Because the difference is one where the race is concerned, and if you make studies of the performance of the Negro child —it was found in a study of 8,000 children in Chicago not long ago, and they were able to find 103 children, Negro children, with intelligence quotients above 120, that is very bright. Now, they had to look through 8,000 to get them, and in a comparable group of 8,000 white children you would get 800 with I.Q.'s above 120 which, to me, shows that the incidence of high intelligence is about 7-8 to 1."

Q. "What about the 103 Negroes that do?"

A. "80% of them are mixed blood."

Q. "How do you know that?"

A. "They said so. I don't know whether they knew it or not, but that's what they said."

---

27. *Stell* Printed Transcript, p. 176.

Q. "Who said it?"

A. "The children, or their parents. It's reported in the report."

Q. "Now, this 2% [overlap] in Savannah, Chatham County, Georgia, would you be in favor of putting them in the white schools?"

A. "No."

Q. "That's what I thought."

A. "Do you know why? You didn't ask me why."

Q. "I think that's obvious."

A. "Because I think they would be miserable and I'm a friend of the children. I don't want to put them in there and hurt them."

Q. Did you ask them whether they would be miserable or not?"

A. "No, and you didn't either."[28]

This completed the Negro cross-examination of Garrett. His testimony had carried the trial into its second day. During the intervening night the usual strenuous conferences and preparations had occurred. No one was sure whether members of the hierarchy were going to appear for the Negroes, but we now began to suspect that they would not—that the NAACP had more confidence in the appellate courts deciding in their favor against all the evidence than they did in the hierarchy surviving cross-examination. It was a contemptuous reliance on an extraordinary coalition.

Early in the proceedings next morning after Dr. Garrett stepped down, George Leonard called to the stand Dr. Clairette Armstrong who had been for two years Professional Chief Psychologist at Bellevue Hospital in New York City. She had run various tests on truancy in the New York schools and testified to the effect of school frustration on runaways. One-third of Negro truants, she had found, were truants by their own admisison because of inability to maintain the standard in integrated classes. In cross-examination Mrs. Motley continued her attack:

Q. [By Mrs. Motley] "Well, let me ask you this: Is it your testimony that Negro children in Chatham County, Georgia,

---

28. For further discussion of the exceptional Negro, see *infra*, pp.87, 90-93, 121-3, 125-6.

should not be admitted to schools with white children because Negroes are inherently inferior?"

A. "Well, the results show that they can't keep up with the averages of the Whites, don't they?"

Q. "That's right, but what's the reason for that?"

A. "I am strongly on the organic side. I think it's an innate, intrinsic ability. Of course, if they were brought up in a vacuum, even the bright ones wouldn't succeed either, but in an average school situation the bright ones show their metal as a rule. . . ."

Q. "Do you think the Negroes are innately inferior to whites, is that your testimony?"

A. "There is a spread, of course, from lowest to highest, but the averages, on the averages, the means are different, so that from my own experience, I would say that it is an inferiority."

Q. "And on what do you base your conclusion that this is due to race?"

A. "The mere fact that it occurs in all the literature and all the statistical studies, in all research, and in my own experience."

Q. "Now, have you made any tests yourself which would show conclusively that this is race alone?"

A. "I just said 'yes.' I would say it is race. There is nothing else that you can attribute it to. The study of 400 delinquent boys that I have quoted, 200 black and 200 whites, or 200 Negroes, 200 whites, have shown it right through scholastically, intelligence, and so forth."

Such was the substance of the Negro cross-examination of Dr. Armstrong on that second, decisive morning. She was excused and a few minutes' recess taken. The crowd in the public benches rose to stretch their legs in the corridors.

I paced the corridors, too, with a sense of approaching climax. The next witness would be Dr. George and, to me at least, this was the crux of the case. In the testimony so far, through the psychology witnesses, everything had been done that could be done in the nature of that subject to refute the Boas dogma. Dr. Garrett had even invaded the field of genetics, citing the Newman-Holzinger study and the study of Sir Cyril Burt with their evidence on the preponderant influence of heredity over environment. But no amount of testimony from these sources could equal in finality an examination of anatomical structure.

This was the *substance* of inheritance, a disclosure of just *what it was* the Negro inherited.

Obviously Mrs. Motley must realize this, and I anticipated that now, if ever, she would be on the warpath—except for one thing. Our case was ironclad, and if she touched it the strength of our position could only be enhanced. This area did not lend itself to any possible conflict of interpretation. Nor was the court a forum for slippery evasions and diversions. The chicanery of the hierarchy would be useless here; so would the undocumented assertions, and the political bombast. All that really remained for Motley now was silence and an implicit faith in her unique alliance.

At last the recess ended and Dr. George took the stand. At the table for counsel for the Negroes, I sensed a certain restlessness. George identified himself and established his qualifications without interruption. Motley was holding her fire.

Next George proceeded, step by step, to survey the relationship between brain weight, body size and intelligence throughout the animal kingdom. He discussed the importance of the prefrontal areas of the brain—"in the porpoise and that group of aquatic mammals the evolutionary increase of brain size is in the sensory lobes, not in the frontal lobes."

Then, still without interruption, he examined the authorities on the function of the pre-frontal areas in man:

Q. [By Mr. Pittman] "What are the higher mental processes, so regarded among scientists?"

A. "Well, would you let me read?"

Q. "Yes, sir, anything with which you agree."

A. "Well, I read recently through my interest in this matter to see what the latest studies by competent neurologists had to say about this. This is a statement from the textbook, 'The Neuro-anatomical Basis for Clinical Neurology,' published in 1961, by Talmadge Peele, who is Neurologist at Duke Medical School. It is the pre-frontal portion of the frontal lobes which are primarily concerned with these higher mental activities according to the evidence that we have. He says: 'The pre-frontal portion of the frontal lobes, while contributing to the elaborateness of movement, bestows upon an individual an ability to plan and to look ahead, a capacity for perceiving a stimulus or problem, not only as an event of the present, but in relation to past experience and anticipation of future possibilities and the ability to maintain a steadfastness of purpose in the face of distractions and an ability to adjust himself agreeably to his neighbors and to control his emotional reactions.' Now, there is Peele's statement, which answers your question and I accept it as mine."

Next George surveyed the findings of Vint and others on the relative weight and structure of White and Negro brains, amid total silence. Perhaps I should say there was silence except for one sound. I was distressed to realize that Constance Motley was weeping audibly.

Q. "Doctor, I will ask you whether or not these differences in brain structures are inherited or are they the result of environment?"

A. "Well, in my mind, there is no doubt that they are inherited."

Q. "Can those differences, in your opinion, be modified by environment?"

A. "To a minimal degree."

Q. "Over what period of time?"

A. "Well, I think that it's possible in the course of a lifetime. Our experiences, of course, affect our brains to some extent. But to increase the inherited basis would require, perhaps, a hundred thousand years to allow time for the concurrences of mutations and the survival of beneficial mutations. We all have brains which we subject to experience and to education and it is reasonable to suppose that education and experience influence to some extent the structures of the brain, but there is no evidence that it increases its mass in any significant degree."

Pittman and George were proceeding methodically through the evidence in spite of the tension in the courtroom. They covered the principal authorities, including Coon.

Q. "Now, Doctor, are you familiar with the writings, or some of the writings, of Dr. Carleton Coon?"

A. "Yes, I have read his *Origin of Races* with a great interest . . ."

Q. "If I may, Doctor, I will read to you an excerpt from pages 115 and 116 . . . and after reading it I will ask you if you agree with him."

A. "All right."

Q. " 'Human beings also vary in temperament. It is a common observation among anthropologists who have worked in many parts of the world in intimate contact with people of differences —people of different races—that racial differences in temperament also exist and can be predicted. Races also differ in the size and weight of endocrine glands, and in the substances carried in the urine. The study of these variations has just begun, and many readers who believe in the current dogma that all behavioral differences are due to man's unique capacity for learning will find this unpalatable, but the burden of proof is on them. If such differences are not related to the endocrine system, then man is indeed a unique animal.' Do you agree with that statement, Doctor?"

A. "I think that is very fundamentally sound, yes."

There could be no turning back now; the examination continued ruthlessly, methodically, with a cumulative impact.

Q. "Doctor, I would like to call your attention to a statement by Dr. James H. Sequeira, which appeared in the March 1932 issue of The British Medical Journal, and ask if you agree with that? . . . Are you familiar with Dr. Sequeira's writing?"

A. "Yes, I have read it in the Journal."

Q. "I will read, now, a portion: 'The average cranial capacity of the European is 1,490 c.cm, while that of the East African is only 1,310 c.cm. The average weight of the brains is set out in the following table:

Caucasoid (meaning white)	1,380 grams.
East African	1,280 grams.
Negroid	1,240 grams.
Australoid	1,180 grams.

"Do you agree with those findings by Dr. Sequeira?"

A. "Yes, I do, give or take a few grams here and there, they have been confirmed by many other studies."

Q. "In that same article, Doctor, . . . I will read this to you; Sequeira says that, according to his findings and that of Dr. Vint's observations, the frontal cortex may be summarized as follows:

'The infragranular layer, East African 106. European 100. The granular layer, East African, 98.7. European 100. The supragranular layer East Africa 92. European 100.' Does that, Doctor, in your opinion, correctly state the difference in measurements of the frontal cortex between the East African and the European according to your studies?"

A. "That is the correct statement that Vint made, and I can only accept his statement, and I have no reason to consider it wrong." [29]

Q. "I continue one further paragraph: 'The infra-granular layer is held to be the seat of the representation—the physical basis—of the animal instincts, reproduction, self-preservation, etc., the granular layer that of the perception of sensations; while the supra-granular layer is concerned with will, intellect, control, etc. The two latter may be looked upon as the physical basis of mind. In the East African, therefore, animal instincts are provided with 6 per cent more physical basis than in the European, but the physical basis of "mind" shows a preponderance in favor of the European of 9.3 per cent.' Now, do you agree with that statement?"

A. "Yes, I do."

So it went on through all the biological evidence. Motley controlled herself in time, but there were no challenges whatever from the NAACP. Nor was one word of cross-examination attempted. At the conclusion of Dr. George's testimony the Transcript read:

Mr. Pittman: "That's all, Doctor."
The Court: "Any questions?"
Mrs. Motley: "No questions, your Honor."
The Court: "Any questions from the Savannah people [the School Board]?"
Mr. Leverett: "No."
The Court: "All right, Doctor. You may step down . . ."

Thus into the record under oath, unchallenged and uncontradicted either by counsel or by opposing witnesses, went the heart of the *Stell* case—damning in its indictment of the scien-

---

29. Dr. George has submitted to me the following footnote to this answer: "The data in the question were evidently taken from Sequeira's report of Vint's preliminary paper (*Kenya and East African Medical Journal*). In essential facts these are in accord with data given in Vint's definitive paper (Vint, 1934, *Journal of Anatomy* 68:216), with one exception: in that definitive paper Vint reports the infra-granular as being thicker in the East African than in the European only in the visuosensory area of the cortex."

tific hierarchy, a stripping-off of decades of deceit and chicanery at the core of public policy, an immediate levy upon the honor of the higher courts.

Anything further in the courtroom now could only be anti-climax.

CHAPTER V

DECISIONS—ON AND OFF THE RECORD

Anti-climax though it seemed to me who had been preoccupied with the central issue, what followed at Brunswick nevertheless had a vital bearing on two collateral points which were constantly arising in the Negro controversy.

The White children's last witness was Dr. Ernest van den Haag, the New York University professor who had unmasked Kenneth Clark. Following Dr. George on the afternoon of May 10 he testified at length concerning the effect upon the exceptional Negro of transfer to integrated schools.

This, the overlap problem, was one of the second lines of defense to which the liberal habitually retreated after defeat on the biological issues, and van den Haag dealt with it exhaustively. He developed the subject of group identification from a psychological standpoint, remarking that "although . . . a superior pupil might possibly identify with other superior pupils of a different group, as a matter of fact, in my experience, the pupil retains his identification with his own group. This identification may lead to certain psychological consequences. . . ."

The point involved, of course, was the integrationists' argument that segregation, whatever might be said for it in the case of the average Negro, was unfair to the superior Negro—that he, at any rate, was entitled to schooling among his White peers. Van den Haag offered material concerning the effect upon *all* Negroes of forced disassociation from their own group and forced integration with a basically different group, a subject which was to be further developed in companion cases to *Stell.*[1]

Again no significant cross-examination occurred. But in the course of what little there was, a point arose which brought the

---

1. See *Brown vs. School District No. 20,* 226 Fed. Supp. 819 (E.D.S.C. 1963), *Evers vs. Jackson School District,* 232 Fed. Supp. 241 (S.D. Miss., 1964); also, Opinion of the Court in *Stell, infra,* pp. 90-91. Also *infra,* pp. 121-2.

Stell case into sharp focus. Several times during the trial, counsel for the Negroes had fallen back on what I might call a sub-division of the undocumented-assertion technique of the hierarchy. It consisted in asking: "Isn't yours the minority view?" It was a form of the one-man-one-vote concept gone berserk and it fitted well into socialism's regimentation philosophy. So I was gratified when van den Haag, too, faced the question and answered it as follows:

Q. "Well, let me ask you this, Doctor: Does your position, as you have testified to here today, does that reflect the majority opinion or the minority opinion?

A. " . . . If you will permit me, I will have to tell you that I have not counted heads on the matter, and the reason I have not counted heads is that it has never appeared to me that scientific questions are decided by a vote, and I know of no one who would today agree to that.

"Let me suggest that when Galileo decided that the earth moves around the sun the majority opinion at that time decided or insisted that the sun moves around the earth, but Galileo was right, though he was a minority of one, and so should I find myself in this minority of one I would not regret it. I have not established what the size of the group is that shares my views or what the size of the group is that holds different views. . . . I don't know whether they amount to the majority, but certainly they include a great number of distinguished men.

"However, *their behavior and my personal contact with them has not convinced me that they have taken their positions on the basis of what they themselves would normally consider as evidence* [emphasis added] and it has also convinced me that they feel sort of a moral duty, right or wrong, to take this position, and feel apparently that to take this position that they are considerably morally better and justifies ignoring and sometimes tailoring scientific evidence."

The matter could hardly have been more tactfully stated. In these words van den Haag drew a thumbnail sketch of a world-wide condition. And he confirmed a prescription for the hypnosis of millions: Indoctrinate a controlling group of scientists in a politically oriented, environmentalist dogma over a period of two generations; make a moral issue out of something immoral; persecute and suppress any dissenters; infiltrate the mass media, and finally persuade the courts by introducing only falsified evidence. Thereafter rely solely, in those courts, on the "majority" view. Never again permit the truth to come to light if you can help it. Thus before my eyes at this trial had unrolled the pattern I had found everywhere else in our national life in almost exact duplication.

The testimony on May 10th virtually ended the trial. There were a few remaining technicalities which were handled at a sitting of the Court at Savannah on May 13, but I did not remain for these. I went home to await the decision.

On June 28 the Court announced its opinion and judgment, together with certain findings, the chief of which were:

"5. The psychometric test results have conclusively demonstrated that the differences between white and negro students in learning capabilities and school performance vary in increasing degree from the pre-school period through the completion of high school. The differences between white and negro students were consistent on all types of tests and increased with chronological age at a predictable and constant rate. The negro overlap of the median white scores dropped from approximately 15% in the lowest grades to 1-2% in the highest and indicated that the negro group reached an educational plateau as much as four years before the white group. When a special control group was selected for identity of age and intelligence quotient in the lower grades, the negro students lagged by two to four years when the entire group reached the 12th grade.

"6. The tests covered general intelligence, reading and arithmetic achievement, and mental maturity. On the last, the white average was 22 points above the negro average. The achievement tests showed major ability pattern differences. On reading comprehension and arithmetic fundamentals there was virtually no overlap between the two groups. . . .

"8. All the evidence before the Court was to the effect that the differences in tests results between the white and negro students is attributable in large part to hereditary factors, predictably resulting from a difference in the races. The evidence establishes and the Court so finds that of the twenty-point difference in maturity test results between negro and white students in Savannah-Chatham County a negligible portion can be attributed to environmental factors. Furthermore no evidence whatsoever was offered to this Court to show that racial integration of the schools could reduce these differences. Substantially all the difference between these two groups of children is inherent in the individuals and must be dealt with by the defendants [the School Board] as an unchangeable factor in programming the schools for the best educational results."

So much for the basic facts. Then the Court turned to a related matter:

"11. The congregation of two substantial and identifiable groups in a single classroom, under circumstances of distinct group identification and varying abilities would lead to conflict impairing the educational process. It is essential for an individual to identify himself with a reference group for healthy personality development. Physical and psychological differences are the common basis of group identification, indeed they compel such self-identification. To increase this divisive tendency, it has been established without contradiction, that selective association is a universal human trait; that physically observable racial differences form the basis for preferential association and that patterns of racial preference are formed and firmly established at a pre-school age.

"12. The effects of intergroup association are reasonably predictable on the basis of that branch of psychology known as social dynamics. In the case of two identifiable groups in the same classroom, intergroup tensions and conflicts result. These become substantial when the groups have a high identification index in a situation where the difference between them is as great as that existing between white and negro children in the Savannah-Chatham County schools."

Finally the Court came to the question of the exceptional Negro:

"15. Throughout the trial, counsel for plaintiffs emphasized the conceded ability of certain superior negro children to meet the progress norms of the white classes and implied that at least selective transfers of such students to white schools would not cause injury similar to the effects of group integration. The Court finds that such selective integration would cause even greater psychological harm to the individual negro children involved and to the balance of their group.

"16. Negro children so transferred would not only lose their right of achievement in their own group but would move to a class where they would be inescapably conscious of total social rejection by the dominant group. Such children must try to identify themselves with the white children while unable to free themselves from continuing identification with other negro children. Additionally, the children involved, while able to maintain the rate of the white class at first, would, according to all of the test results, thereafter tend to fall further back in each succeeding term.

"17. The effects on the remaining negro children would be even more injurious. The loss of the better group members would greatly increase any existing sense of inferiority. The competitive drive to educational accomplishment for those not transferred would be taken away. The Court finds that selective integration would cause substantial and irremovable psychological injury both to the individual transferee and to other negro children."

In view of these and other findings, the Court not unreasonably rendered judgment in favor of the White children; perhaps it would be more accurate to say in favor of all the children. The injunction prayed for by the NAACP was denied and their complaint dismissed.

I could also add parenthetically that no meaningful discussion of the case occurred in any newspaper of national influence.[2] The Opinion and Judgment dropped into a deep well of silence.

So now nothing remained but to await the NAACP appeal to the Fifth Circuit Court of Appeals. A hearing before that court was held on April 9, 1964, in Atlanta. I was not present, but some who were informed me that the smouldering anger of certain of the judges was ill-concealed. I could guess that it was the kind of anger often characteristic of men faced with a moral challenge beyond their capacity to meet.

Then on June 18 came their decision. It reversed the trial court, ignoring the evidence entirely. First they said: "We reiterate that no inferior federal court may refrain from acting as required by that decision [the decision of the Supreme Court in *Brown*]

---

2. One magazine, *U.S. News and World Report,* on May 27, 1963, carried a brief commentary.

even if such a court should conclude that the Supreme Court
erred either as to its facts or as to the law." Thus they transferred all responsibility concerning the evidence to the Supreme
Court. But they could not resist the following characteristic
aside on the subject of overlap:

"The real fallacy, Constitution-wise, of the classification theory
is that many of the Negro pupils overlap many of the white
pupils in achievement and aptitude but are nevertheless to be
segregated on the basis of race. They are to be separated, regardless of how great their ability as individuals, into schools
with members of their own race because of the difference in
test averages as between the races. Therein is the discrimination.
The individual Negro student is not to be treated as an individual and allowed to proceed along with other individuals on
the basis of ability alone without regard to race."

All too obviously the Court here was ignoring Dr. van den
Haag's testimony on this precise point and the findings upon
it of the Court below. It looked suspiciously, to counsel and
to me, as if the Court had not even read them. But what was
worse, it here gave as one reason for its decision a concept
which, if generally applied, would disrupt our society. It was in
effect holding unconstitutional any law which disadvantaged
any individual belonging to a group whose average performance
justified that law.

For example, state statutes limiting working hours for women
in factories had been held constitutional because the average
woman was not as strong as the average man, and in spite of
the fact that certain women were stronger than many men. Would
the Fifth Circuit in such a case now paraphrase its racial holding
to read: "The real fallacy, Constitution-wise, of the classification
theory is that many women overlap many men in strength but
are nevertheless to be segregated on the basis of sex. They are
to be forbidden to work, regardless of how great their strength
as individuals or their financial need, because of the difference
in the average endurance of the two sexes."

Or one could take the case of the exceptional minor who was
not allowed to vote, drive a car or marry simply because the

average minor was not considered wise, or experienced, or mature enough to do these things. Certainly many minors had better judgment, more experience and more intelligence than many adults. Would the Fifth Circuit now paraphrase themselves and say: "The real fallacy, Constitution-wise, of the classification theory is that many minors overlap many adults in judgment and intelligence but are nevertheless to be segregated on the basis of age. They are to be denied the right to vote, to drive and to marry regardless of how great their judgment and intelligence as individuals, because of the limitations of the average minor. Therein is the discrimination. The individual minor is not to be treated as an individual and allowed to proceed along with other individuals on the basis of ability alone without regard to age."

Restating these situations in the Fifth Circuit's own words seemed to make the invalidity of their reasoning sufficiently clear. It would be disastrous to compel society to accept the burden of the average child at the voting booth or automobile license bureau in order to satisfy the exceptional child, and it was proving equally disastrous to accept the average Negro in White schools in order to satisfy the exceptional Negro. To damage a whole society with torrents of injurious influences in order to accommodate the exceptional few was something new even to socialism.

In fact in reading the opinion of the Fifth Circuit Court of Appeals I had to pinch myself to believe I was not dreaming. I seemed to be wandering in some sort of judicial Alice in Wonderland. But the last straw, say rather the last blow, was yet to come. The White children took the reversal by the Fifth Circuit to the Supreme Court by a petition for a writ of *certiorari,* and the long wait for its final ruling started.

Six months later it came. I remembered well the afternoon it was expected. I was in telephone communication with Leonard. We waited hardly knowing whether to hope or despair. What possible reason could the Supreme Court give for ignoring decisive and uncontradicted evidence with a fundamental bearing upon both a nation's domestic welfare and a total world situation?

The least the Court could do, we thought, would be to remand the case to the trial court for a rehearing in which the NAACP would be required to put the hierarchy on the witness stand. In that way the entire subject could be even more glaringly exposed. It hardly seemed proper to ask: did the Supreme Court dare? How could it possibly do otherwise when to fail would have such shattering implications?

Not only were Leonard and I waiting for the ruling. The attorneys general of seven states had filed a petition with the Court asking that *certiorari* be granted. Besides this, during the interval since the decision in the Fifth Circuit, the trial court in *Evers,* ' acting on even more complete evidence than had been offered in *Stell,* had closed its opinion with the following paragraph:

"In the opinion of this Court, the facts in this case point up a most serious situation, and, indeed, 'cry out' for a reappraisal and complete reconsideration of the findings and conclusions of the United States Supreme Court in the *Brown* decision, as interpreted by the United States Court of Appeals for the Fifth Circuit. Accordingly, this Court respectfully urges a complete reconsideration of the decision in the *Brown* case."

Suddenly my telephone rang. I picked up the receiver and heard Leonard's voice. The news from the Supreme Court had just come in. *Certiorari* in *Stell* was denied. There was no explanation, no comment. There would be no rehearing, no further proceedings.

Stell had dropped into a deeper chasm than any well of silence. The appeal to truth, the levy upon honor, had failed.

---

3. On July 6, 1964, the trial court in *Evers* had felt compelled, against what it found to be the weight of the evidence, to decide for the NAACP, because of the prior ruling of the Fifth Circuit in *Stell*. The final farce in this circus of absurdity was reached in the opinion of the Fifth Circuit on Jan. 26, 1966, confirming the decision in *Evers* in favor of the Negroes, and offering a new excuse for its action. This argument is considered *infra*, pp. 141-2.

CHAPTER VI

POINT COUNTER-POINT

Mechanically I replaced my legal folder in my brief case. For the moment the memories and the anger made me forget the detachment of Seal Harbor. In that folder was something from which none of us who had any part in it could ever again be detached.

The clock in the hall struck three. I turned wearily from my desk and started for bed, but half way to the door I paused. I could not shake off the haunting need to find a key—an explanation of the nightmare.

In my brief case was one last folder, one which I sometimes called my nest of needles. It contained, among other things, a variety of questions, usually but not always hostile, that had reached me in the course of the years since *Race and Reason* was published. Many had come by mail, although probably the majority were gleaned from question-and-answer sessions following speeches I had made at various universities. One group I remembered by rote because they arose so often in social situations among liberals in the nation's capital where I lived.

Taken as a whole, these questions covered a wide range of issues related but somewhat peripheral to the main thread of my evening's meditations. They represented in most cases the reactions, the confusions, and the doubts of a bewildered public. Some were obvious attempts to evade reality. But all in one way or another were provocative. Possibly from a consideration of these might emerge an answer to the broader question I was asking myself.

So out from the nest came the needles, and I attempted to arrange them, together with my replies, in some logical order:

Your activities acerbate the situation. Why don't you offer a solution instead of increasing tensions?

No permanent solution to any problem was ever found without going to the heart of it. The heart of the Negro problem lies in establishing the correct answer to one question, namely, are the Negro's limitations the result of his bad environment or is his bad environment the result of his limitations? Can we, by making every effort to improve the Negro's surroundings and education, reach the root cause of his comparative performance, or is it a matter of innate racial differences?

Every public policy concerning race will be decided differently depending on the answer given to that question. Obviously it will, as regards education. Can you not see that it also will, as regards housing, slum clearance, and job opportunities? And what about foreign policy? What about the administration of aid to under-developed countries, what about giving "freedom" to African Negroes? Is it not clear that in all of these vital areas, if the answer is environment, policies will be the direct opposite of what they will be if the answer is genetics?

Now consider our present predicament. We are forming every one of our programs on the environmental hypothesis, in spite of the fact that all the evidence is to the effect that this hypothesis is wrong. What, then, can be more imporant than correcting the hypothesis and starting to form policies on reality instead of on illusion? There is no other road to a solution. What you are seeking are not solutions. You are really looking for sleeping pills.

Yours is a gospel of hate. You must be tired of controversy and bitterness. Why not try love for a change?

I never hated anything in my life except two things: dishonesty and the appeasement of evil. These I hate with every fiber of my being. I would rather face controversy and bitterness indefinitely than surrender to either one.

Let me also point out that among hard-core leftists and race agitators (as distinguished from bemused humanitarians) the real source of hatred is envy, and you know on which side it originates.

If we can't believe the scientists on race differences, who can we believe?

It is not a question of disbelieving scientists in general. It is a question of disbelieving the current scientific hierarchy, examining the statements of its members critically, noting their political, non-scientific nature and their lack of documentation, observing their constant avoidance of the actual evidence, and then of turning to other scientists who present such evidence.

No intelligent person who does this in the context of our times can come to any conclusion other than that the hierarchy is deceiving the public for political purposes. The situation is so plain it is almost ludicrous. Unfortunately it does take a little reading and comparing, some ability to resist accepting the most publicized view one hears.

ANTHROPOLOGY

You cited a UNESCO study to substantiate that Negroes mature earlier than Whites. Please re-study the finding of this work. The reasons for early maturation of the Negro were due to climatic differences of their environment and not for biological reasons. Negroes in the same climate as the Whites mature at the same rate.

This question confuses the age of sexual maturation with a *kinesthetic* maturation process during the first months of life. The difference between White and Negro *kinesthetic* maturation is not due to climate since (1) Kampala, Uganda, where the tests were made is 2500 feet above sea level and (2) in their 1957 paper Geber and Dean[1] studied 15 European babies and 60 Indian babies in the same environment as the African babies. The European and Indian babies gave the same results as had been found in Europe.

Psychological tests of a child's "I.Q." at an early age measure motor ability and advanced motor ability is not considered

---

1. "Development Rates of African Children in Uganda," *The Lancet* (June 15, 1957), *272*, No. 6981, pp. 1216-1219.

indicative of low I.Q. In fact, the correlation between motor ability at an early age and mental I.Q. at a late one is so low as to be considered not significant. Which facts—yours or mine—are right?

I have stated my sources; you do not state yours. Geber found a significantly faster kinesthetic maturation rate in Negro infants than in White infants.[2] Almost all investigators have found a significantly lower I.Q. on the average among older Negroes than among older Whites. It is likewise well known that rapid maturation of the neuromuscular system is characteristic of the lower animals. What kind of correlation does this suggest to you?

The subject may be worth a brief background examination. We have in man and the higher animals two neural pathways that control our coordinated motor functions. These two systems are the *pyramidal* and the *extrapyramidal*. They have a considerable degree of independence structurally and functionally but they have interconnections and they collaborate in executing our mature complex motor functions.

The extrapyramidal system is the old motor system. It is composed largely of cells located in deep gray matter of the cerebral hemispheres. They have some connections with the cortex. This deep gray matter of the *corpus striatum* (unusually highly developed in birds) presides over production and control of instinctive and some other automatic movements.

The pyramidal system is our new motor system. The cells of origin of its transmission fibers are located in the cortex, and impulses pass directly to effector nerve cells that stimulate muscle fibers. The function of the pyramidal system is to originate and transmit impulses that arise in the realm of awareness and produce precise voluntary movements. Not only is this the last motor system to arise in the evolutionary process, it is the last to mature in individual life.

In lower forms the extrapyramidal motor system is dominant and quite effective, but as it has evolved in the evolutionary series

----

2. For example, the uterine Moro reflex was found to disappear in White children on the average between the 8th and 12th *weeks* of life, but with all the 107 Negro children it disappeared before the 5th *day* of life.

of vertebrates this system has lost some of its independent effi-
ciency. In man the pyramidal system is dominant, although co-
ordination with the old extrapyramidal system seems necessary for
effective action. In the human newborn the pyramidal system is
immature and has not yet come into effective function; at the same
time the extrapyramidal system has become subordinate in some
degree to the pyramidal system. Hence, the perfection of many
motor functions must await the maturation of the pyramidal
system.

The facts presented by Geber and Dean suggest a greater reten-
tion in African babies of the primitive independence of the extrapyramidal system. This could account for the motor precosity of
Negro babies. There is evidence for the hypothesis that the more
primitive, greater independence of the extrapyramidal system of
Africans is associated with a more primitive condition of the cortex. In addition to the now widely known observations of Vint
on the supragranular layers, van Noort found the cellular structure of some regions of the cortex to present a different appearance in the Caucasian and Negro races.[3] I stated that this is one
of the areas where the *balance* of the evidence has to be considered. I do not say in this case the data is conclusive. I say it is
suggestive.

As to early intelligence tests, Dr. Geber, using Gesell Development Quotients, found distinct superiority among Negro children
until the third year, thereafter distinct inferiority. These tests
measure more complex muscular performance and probably com-
bine simple reflexes with much more complex, cerebrally learned
behavior.

*Assuming for the moment that you are correct re: the racial
inferiority of the Negro, why is it necessary to believe that inter-*

---

3. C. U. Ariens Kappers, G. Carl Huber, Elizabeth Crosby, *The Comparative Anatomy of the Nervous System of Vertebrates, Including Man,*
1936, New York, p. 1632. For the significance of differences in the pyramidal cells, see A. F. and R. F. Tredgold, *Manual of Psychological Medicine,* 3rd ed., 1953, London, p. 254.

marriage would necessarily lower the quality of human beings produced and thus the quality of American civilization? That is, why assume that Negro inferior traits are dominant? Why not assume, as the human evolutionary process suggests, that superior traits are dominant, and thus intermarriage would have the effect of raising the total quality of American civilization?

It is not necessary to believe *every* mixed mating would lower the quality of human being produced. If a Negro of superior genetic quality were to interbreed with a genetically poor White their offspring might be superior to the poor White parent.[4]

However, we are not confronted with exceptional individuals only. We are confronted with twenty million Negroes. Scientific evidence and practical experience regarding the intelligence of large unselected groups, and their creative achievements, show that Negroes as a group, in this country and across the world, have appreciably lower average intelligence scores and a vastly lower creative record throughout history. If we absorb twenty million largely uncreative Negroes into our White gene pool, the mixed product may be expected to lack the combination of qualities (insight, foresight, intelligence and drive) necessary to maintain and advance American civilization.

Traits may be desirable or undesirable; also they may be dominant or recessive. We cannot rely upon undesirable traits being recessive or desirable traits being dominant. Achondroplastic dwarfism is undesirable and dominant. Undesirable traits are frequently dominant.

It is of course true that natural selection tends to eliminate those traits which are biologically disadvantageous in a particular environment. This, however, is a factor which has little chance to operate in a society subsidizing the poor.

How could the Negro have evolved from Homo erectus 30,000 years ago, when no fossils of this type younger than 200,000 years old are known?

---

4. For a contrary view see "Significant Evidence on Inheritance and Hybridization, Part I", 1966, G. Pantel, *Mankind Quarterly*, Vol. 6, No. 4, pp. 219-238.

Your facts are incorrect. A Negroid *Homo erectus* specimen dated about 30,000 years ago was found at Broken Hill, Northern Rhodesia, in 1921.[5] There is a fairly good continuity of *erectus* and *sapiens* skeletons in Africa. The oldest *sapiens* skulls found there appear to be a set of four which Leakey excavated in Kenya in 1932; their exact age is controversial but they are probably in the general range of the Broken Hill specimen.

The Eskimo has a larger brain than the White man. This disproves the importance of brain size as a measure of racial intelligence. Comment?

How does it disprove it? In the first place, you supply no data on the "other-things-being-equal" aspect of this case. You offer no study of the relative sulcification or proportion of parts of the Eskimo brain.

Nor have you provided evidence on the relative intelligence of the Eskimo, relying entirely, it would seem, on the Eskimo's primitive culture. However, the Eskimo's adaptation to his environment is remarkable. He invented the skin boat, the dome and the best cold-proof clothes in the world. He is regarded by the Air Force on the DEW line as an excellent mechanic.

Possibly the Eskimo has failed to build a civilization because of the rigors of his surroundings. The Eskimo belongs to the Mongoloid race. This race had produced great cultures in the Orient. Some substocks of the Mongoloid once produced great cultures in Central and South America. Others like the North American Indians failed to do so. The point is that both the Caucasoid and Mongoloid races have produced advanced civilizations, in spite of the existence of relict groups among them. The Negro has never produced a great civilization any time, anywhere.

As I have already said, the anatomical and physiological equipment of a race, including the brain, may be likened to tinder which may, or may not, catch fire when brought in contact with a civilization, depending on a variety of circumstances. The tinder

---

5. Carleton S. Coon, *The Story of Man*, 1962, New York, pp. 34-35.

of the Caucasoid and Mongoloid have caught fire often enough to prove their relative susceptibility in any comparison with the Negro.

How about the brain of Neanderthal man?   Was it not as large as the modern Caucasoid?

Here again we shall never be able to make a histological examination of the Neanderthal brain nor a study of its sulcification. Nor can we give a Neanderthal intelligence tests.   According to Coon, the frontal areas of his brain were small since the forehead was very low and slanted.[6]

Some studies in Baltimore recently showed that White and Negro infants up to 40 weeks revealed no differences.   Obviously, therefore, differences thereafter are due to socio-economic factors. What is your answer?

To repeat, the lower centers of the brain and nervous system, in human beings and in animals, are the ones which mature first; the higher centers mature last.   Therefore similarity of performance in the early stages of life signifies nothing as to adult potentiality.

Was not the brain of Anatole France unusually small, although he was a brilliant man?

Anatole France lived to an advanced age and his brain was, of course, examined after death.   Under the circumstances senility had taken its toll.   The human brain has been estimated to lose cells at the rate of 30,000 per day from birth to the end of life.[7]

Moreover in France's brain the cerebrum had marked asymmetry.   The convolutions were long and tortuous, and the foldings were unusually complex.   This and other peculiarities provided considerably more intellectual potential than the brain weight would indicate.[8]

It cannot be too strongly emphasized that brain weight is a

---

6. Carleton Coon, *The Origin of Races, op. cit.*, 529-530.

7. John E. Pfeiffer, "How the Human Memory Functions," 1963, *Think*, 29:6-10; published by I.B.M.

8. L. Guillon *et al, Bulletin Academie de Medecine*, XCI, 1927, 328-36.

criterion of intelligence only in dealing with group averages, never in dealing with individuals. For example, I understand there is now a theory that the hemispheres of the brain may resemble the kidneys or the lungs in that one hemisphere may act as a "spare" for the other if one fails. If this should prove true, then a large weight loss in parts of an individual brain may not be accompanied by any significant loss of intelligence in that individual.

We must concentrate on the group and the average in brain weight studies. We have enough studies of the Negro brain, under varied enough circumstances, to speak with assurance of its relative weight. When this factor is combined with studies of its other features, such as sulcification of the cortex and thickness of the supragranular layer, we can also speak with assurance of its relative evolutionary status.

Are you not aware that man alone is capable of culture and that cultural influences counteract and invalidate all your animal analogies and your references to evolutionary structure?

This question contains a *non sequitur*. It is true that man alone is capable of culture but it does not follow that these influences overbalance structure. On the contrary we have seen that in the case of human beings heredity overbalances environment by a ratio of about three to one. This is just another way of saying that structure overbalances culture by the same ratio.

To revert to the tinder analogy, the Negro has failed, repeatedly and invariably, to respond to the flame of advanced cultures while other races and substocks have responded in varying degrees. Perhaps it would be more accurate to say that the Negro has responded in a lower degree than the White or Yellow races, since obviously civilization will have some effect on any race capable of understanding language. We note by observation and historical experience the performance of the Negro—we see the situation in Africa, Haiti, and our own slums and schools—we see countless cases of opportunity forfeited and of advantages lost. Then we examine structure and we discover the explanation. Culture can only ignite flammable tinder. It cannot make tinder flammable if it is not.

Remember this point whenever you hear an integrationist talk about the "cultural deprivation" which the Negro has suffered. The expression has become a cliché to account for all the Negro's limitations. It is meaningless because you cannot speak of depriving a race of something it is, on the average, incapable of possessing.

There are no such things as pure races. We are all a mixture of many strains—does this not make it meaningless to talk about race?

Not in the least. Race is a very convenient general term and, using it in its widest sense, we may say that there are three broad subdivisions of the human species, the White, the Yellow and the Black. Anthropologists go further—usually to the point of five subdivisions which they have named Caucasoid (White), Mongoloid (Yellow), Congoid (Sudanese, Forest, Negrito and Bantu Blacks), Capoid (Yellow-Black), and Australoid (Yellow-Brown). One may then go on to subdivide these into as many as 31 substocks or strains representing various degrees of intermixture of the above larger divisions.[9]

All of the divisions represent some degree of difference in innate characteristics, distinguishable by observation of physical form. In other words, the differences are genetic and indicate the presence of characteristic genes. In comparing the English-speaking White man (an amalgam of certain substocks of the Caucasoid) and the American Negro (West African Congoid) we are confronted with almost opposite poles of the human racial spectrum. Here are not just differences between substocks inside one of the broader divisions—these are differences between two of the largest human categories and, as we have seen, they represent differences of position on the evolutionary scale as well.

I do not mean that these cannot be mixed and produce something somewhere between, or that they have not been mixed, both in Africa, the Western Hemisphere and elsewhere. I mean that if

---

9. See, for example, Carleton S. Coon and Edward E. Hunt, Jr., Editors, *Anthropology A to Z*, 1963, New York, pp. 119-129.

we can speak of the typical Congoid Negro as the genetic essence of the Black, and the English-speaking Northwestern European Caucasian as a fair example of the White, then basically we are coming almost as close to comparing oil and water as is possible with human beings.

One does not have to have the Negro gene complex in undiluted form to make its presence recognizable and significant. If the most typical of all Congoid Negroes has certain genetic limitations, then any admixture of his genes will carry a proportional degree of limitation in the resulting combination.

Since "lower" races have a common origin and common gene pool from "superior" races, what selective factors have inhibited their (inferior) culture? If you think there are some genetic factors for culture, are these acquired traits? If they are not acquired characteristics they cannot be individual racial traits, since all Homo sapiens have their genes from a common ancestor.

You are hopelessly confused. Genetic factors cannot be acquired. If you want to find out how species and races evolve in plants, animals and man, read a good book on evolution such as Ernst Mayr's *Animal Species and Evolution, 1963,* Cambridge.

It seems doubtful that all races of *Homo sapiens* had a common *Homo erectus* ancestor. According to Coon and Gates the five major races of man branched off from their *Homo erectus* ancestors at different periods and places.

Where did you obtain your erroneous material relating to the cerebral area of the dolphin's brain—advise that you refer to the work being conducted by the University of Calif. School of Veterinary Medicine — Neurological Anatomy, Davis Campus. What Society? What university? What publisher? Is it, or is it not true that the dolphin has both a larger cerebral area and a more complex convolution pattern than the white man—why not legislate in their field too?

While it is true that dolphins have a more complex convolutional pattern than man and perhaps a larger area of cerebral cortex, I have repeatedly pointed out that such facts by themselves do not determine relative intelligence nor evolutionary grade. In the case of the dolphin, other facts are more significant: specifically, the cortex of these animals is primitive in cellular architecture, the supragranular layer is thin, and the frontal association areas are absent.[10]

Although there are differences in weight, relative sizes of fissures, numbers of neurons found in the supragranular layers, and "statistical average" differences in the weight of brains between the races, have these differences, by scientific experiments, been shown to be directly related to an individual's capacity to learn?

They have been shown to be related to evolutionary status and evolutionary status is certainly related to capacity to learn. For specific relations of parts to functions, look at Penfield and Rasmussen.[11]

Concerning the origin of man, do the findings of Leakey in the Rift Valley (East Africa) in any way contradict your postulate concerning the duration of development of races?

No. Leakey's 1961 find is about 14 million years old; his Australopithecines date from about 300,000 to 1,500,000 years ago. Thus they overlapped *Homo erectus* somewhat but vanished from the earth long before the *erectus-sapiens* transition.

What are your biological qualifications for the biological interpretations of this rather biased presentation? It has to be a biological (genetic) interpretation to be a racial characteristic. Biased literature = biased reasoning.

------

10. See G. R. Langworthy, "A description of the central nervous system of the porpoises," *Journal of Comparative Neurology*, 1932, Vol. 54. In the most recent study of the dolphin brain the authors speak of the drastic curtailment of the frontal lobe and state that there is almost no cortex anterior to the genu of the corpus callosum. See P. J. Morgane and P. I. Yakovlev, "Surface configurations of the forebrain and cortical areas in the bottlenose dolphin, tursiops truncatus," *Anatomical Record*, 1966, Vol. 154, p. 390. This research comes from the Division of Neurological Sciences, Communication Research Institute, Miami, Fla., and the Department of Neuropathology, Harvard Medical School.

11. *Supra,* pp. 49-50.

I have a science degree, as well as a law degree, but I have never pretended to be a professional scientist or a specialist in racial matters. What I have done is listen to both sides and read materials presented by both sides — at the same time noting the efforts by the scientific hierarchy to suppress and distort evidence and to persecute other scientists who offer material exploding the equalitarian dogma. Then I have tried to call the attention of the public to what is going on.

You quote Coon as stating, "Brain size is related to achievement." Is it not well documented that achievement (economic, academic, artistic, and managerial) is dependent on much more than innate intelligence?

I have mentioned the probability that the development of the frontal lobes has a relation to planning, foresight and motivation—the *use* of intelligence. If this be true, then the brain is still involved in many attributes which might not be called intelligence in the narrowest sense.

Beyond this we may say that a man's character is the product not only of his brain and entire nervous system but also of his glands and internal secretions, which interact with his nervous system. Negroes differ from Whites in these secretions[12]

Finally, there is that one-quarter contribution by environment. But with full allowance for these things, it still remains true that brain size is *related* to achievement. There is no contradiction.

Ralph Linton in The Tree of Culture makes reference to the fact that certain Negro tribes in Africa were in the iron age long before Caucasians in Europe had reached a similar stage of development, being still on a level of stone age civilization.

I have not read Mr. Linton's book but I am advised that while he does say that some African tribes engaged early in simple operations with iron, he does not know whether this occurred before similar activities in Europe. The facts as I understand them are as follows:

---

12. Coon, *The Origin of Races, op. cit.,* pp. 115-116 and works there cited.

Iron smelting was discovered in the general area of Caucasus-Anatolia around 1500 B.C., quickly was adopted by the Hittites and Assyrians, and spread thence to Egypt and the trade ports of the Mediterranean, both African and European. It developed in the interior of Northern Africa near Meroe around 400 B.C. The question, therefore, is whether those responsible can fairly be described as "Negro tribes."

Meroe is on the Nile about 100 miles north of Khartoum in what is now the Sudan. It was part of the viceroy of Kush, ruled by Egypt until the breakdown of New Kingdom power *circa* 1000 B.C. Kush and Meroe were next occupied and governed by an Assyrian military force, equipped with iron armor and weapons. Then in 591 B.C., a force of Greek mercenaries, with iron weapons, appeared in the area and seized part of the region. Apparently, Meroe was the most important iron-producing area of North Africa between about 400 B.C. and 350 A.D.

The reasons to believe Meroe was not Negro are: (a) it is described as "the main southern bastion of Egyptian influence" and as "the southern capital of the kingdom of the Ethiopian kings of Napata from 700 to 300 B.C." [13] The Ethiopians at the time were not Negroes; they were Hamites ruled by Semitic immigrants from southern Arabia. (b) We find at Meroe baths, temples to Isis, Apiremak and the sun, pyramids, stelae of Queen Candace and Akiniras and a head of Octavius. The inscriptions are in Egyptian hieroglyphics and in Meroitic (a debased form of Egyptian), also some fragmentary Greek. All of which shows that the Meroites were not Negro, but culturally and linguistically Egyptian, Greek and Roman." [14]

Is it not true   that because of the great amount of unexplored territory, evidence will be found of an earlier conversion from Homo erectus *to* Homo sapiens? *Is it also not true that the climatic differences between Europe and Africa make the pos-*

---

13. Leonard Cottrell, article on Meroe, *The Concise Encyclopedia of Archaeology*, 1960, London.

14. Dr. Robert Gayre writes me, "Meroe was Cushitic, not Negroid, with Caucasoid overlays, some of them Semitic."

sibility of remains being preserved in Africa much less likely than in Europe?

New evidence may modify our conclusions, not only with respect to the date of the *sapiens-erectus* threshold among Negroes, but in all areas of science. Meanwhile we cannot and should not refuse to judge probabilities from the evidence at hand.

More specifically, it is improbable that the date of the emergence of *Homo sapiens* among Negroids in Africa will be pushed back very far for this reason: As a rule, *Homo sapiens* eliminated the earlier *erectus* types. We have a quite recent *erectus* type in Africa, namely Broken Hill man (Rhodesia) dating from 30,000 B.C. It seems probable that *sapiens* types in Africa, had they emerged at about the date of *sapiens* emergence in Europe or Asia, would have spread over the more habitable portions of the continent and eliminated the *erectus* type tens of thousands, if not hundreds of thousands, of years earlier.

The fact that fire was discovered in Negro Africa only 40,000 years ago as against 250,000 years ago in western Europe and 360,000 years ago in China, based on evidence now available,[15] tends further to support the hypothesis of a much later *erectus-sapiens* transition among Negroids than among Caucasoids and Mongoloids.

Your belief that the climate of Africa makes skeleton preservation more difficult may be valid in some areas. Of 312 fossil man sites enumerated by Coon, 49% are in western Europe, 11% in eastern Europe and the U.S.S.R., 4.5% in East Asia, 7.1% in North Africa, 7.1% in Africa south of the Sahara. But the extent of digging in densely populated areas for building and industrial purposes also has a bearing on the matter. Sometimes it results in finding fossils, sometimes in the fossils being destroyed. Likewise it must be remembered that Africa is a large continent and has a great variety of climate. Finally there have been vast changes in climate in both Europe and Africa in the last 300,000 years.

How is the Government of Liberia so stable?

---

15. Coon, *The Story of Man, op. cit.*, pp. 60-63.

Because it is essentially a political dictatorship, supported economically by Firestone and the Bona Hills Iron mines. Although Liberia was founded by supposedly freedom-loving Negroes from America, the League of Nations was obliged to intervene in 1930 to stop the slave trade. It was found that the President and some of his highest officials were implicated. The President had to resign.

John Gunther in his *Inside Africa* makes some pertinent observations: The people are "mercilessly exploited." A country the size of Ohio, Liberia has 10 miles of paved roads. "Only two native Liberians have ever become doctors." More than 90 per cent of the population is illiterate. Infant mortality in some areas runs as high as 75 per cent. Flagrant corruption exists on all levels.

Gunther finds that prisoners in the jails are either fed by their friends and relatives or starve to death; the budget provision for their keep is devoured by grafting officials. About 15,000 Americo-Liberians rule 1,500,000 Negro natives. The True Whig Party has held power since the 1870's. People who criticize the President are arrested "on any charge."

They have been telling us at Princeton that Brazil is a good example of a multi-racial society and one which we should not hesitate to emulate. Do you agree?

No doubt Brazil satisfies the Brazilians and I have no desire to criticize it. Perhaps Brazilians would not care to see Brazil become another United States, and, I dare say, the average American would not care to see the United States become another Brazil.

The greatest concentration of Negro genes in Brazil is in the Northeast, by far the most backward part of the nation. The most advanced portions of the country are in the Southeast where the Negro population is smallest.

However, taking Brazil as a whole and comparing it with the United States, we find the following:

	Brazil	United States
Life expectancy at birth	35-40 years	67 years
Estimated percent of adults illiterate	51	3-4
Paper consumption per capita (mostly newsprint)	3.6 kg.	36.3 kg.
Gross National Product per capita	$200.00	$2,813.00

The above indices are useful in measuring progress because they lend themselves readily to statistical statement. Political stability and government fiscal responsibility are less easy to compare in figures, but I can assure you Brazil does not rate any higher in this area than it does in the preceding items. All of these points should be called to the attention of your professors when they suggest we follow in Brazil's footsteps.

You say Negro illegitimacy has a rate of 19-22. Most South American countries have rates higher than this. Venezuela has a rate of almost 70. You may ascribe this to mongrelization of the races. How about Mexico, which has few Negroes and has a rate of 22.5? And Argentina, which has a still higher rate, and has a pure white population?

In many Latin American countries high illegitimacy rates exist, but this simply means that stable families have omitted the marriage ceremony. Reasons may include geographical isolation, ignorance, local custom, scarcity of priests or high cost of the marriage service. Illegitimacy *per se* is often determined by social and economic factors and is not too meaningful.[16]

American Negro illegitimacy, on the other hand, occurs in a society in which the Latin American factors are largely non-operative. More significant is the fact that it generally reflects a broken family, in which the man plays a sexual, but not a responsibly paternal, role, in which the mother is the head of the household and the children lack necessary discipline.

a. *Haitian dictators get chopped up. So do Italian and German ones (and even ancient Roman ones). Comment?*

b. *A sociologist who makes a study in which he declares he compared Whites and Negroes who had environmental equality is not*

---

16. An expert on the legal aspect of this subject writes me: "In Latin America common law marriages are the normal type of marriage, but because the Roman Catholic Church's influence is dominant, and so it is impossible to get the legal system to agree to recognize such marriages, the offspring are technically illegitimate. But they are not illegitimate in the eyes of anyone who views the matter from the standpoint of common law or the civil law, but only of canon law."

worth his Ph.D. Negroes are not allowed to have environmental equality in this country, anywhere. They are always subject to discrimination. Comment?

a. The difference is in the frequency and regularity.

b. The phrase used is "as far as possible". You are correct that we cannot completely "equate" without turning the Negro into a White man which is biologically impossible. The point is that as you *approach* equality of environment the gap does not decrease. Note also, that when you equate for background your Negro comes from a higher level of his population than does the White.

T. Dobzhansky, foremost authority on genetics (Genetics & Origin of Species, Mankind Evolving, etc.) states burden of proof is on racists to prove their superiority. There is none. Do you dispute authorities with your biased statements and expect intelligent people to take your word over theirs?

Speaking of bias, I confess to a certain bias against Dobzhansky, a specialist in fruit flies and a man whom I have found dedicated to the political use of science for equalitarian ends. Dobzhansky, a Russian immigrant who taught zoology and genetics in Soviet universities from 1922 to 1927, belongs to the Columbia University equalitarian coterie of proteges and followers of Boas, a group which includes Margaret Mead; Gene Weltfish, who accused the United States of using germ warfare in Korea; and Ashley Montagu, who has been frequently connected as a speaker or sponsor with organizations later cited as Communist.

While none of these circumstances reflect on Dobzhansky's scientific ability, or on that of the other persons named, they suggest a chance of bias on *their* part. In fact, Dobzhansky's attacks on Coon's *Origin of Races* are singularly unconvincing.[17] Therefore, when he says that the burden of proof is on "racists" to prove "their" superiority, I find the assertion pathetic. The burden of proof is upon those who would contradict all previously accepted fact and experience, and who would alter all previously established custom.

As for the evidence itself, there is no evidence for equality.

---

17. See *supra,* p. 54n.

If the Negro is so different genetically, why is it that most Negroes raised in our segregated system cannot qualify for our colleges while many foreign Negroes can qualify to compete in our colleges?

Foreign-born Negroes are skimmed off the top of their intelligence distribution. They are the cream of Negro Africa. When we consider a race we are obliged to speak in averages, not exceptions. Nevertheless you may be interested in looking at the *National Review Bulletin* for February 2, 1965, p. 3, commenting upon a report of a study commission on education and world affairs endowed in 1962 by the Ford and Carnegie Foundations. This report was based upon a survey of 75,000 foreign students on American campuses—55,000 of them from Africa and Asia. The *Bulletin* finds the report "overwhelmingly negative" and goes on to say that too many of the students "are (1) ill prepared scholastically and linguistically for American college courses, (2) intellectually below college level, (3) unwilling to work, and (4) a headache, in the aggregate, to host colleges."

Perhaps of more importance, Clark and Plotkin reported that, on the basis of a study of 1278 Northern college students, those Negroes from Southern segregated schools did better than Negroes from Northern integrated schools.[18]

Bennett and Diamond have made studies at the University of California at Berkeley which prove that an enriched environment changes the measurements of the cortex of rats. Does not this disprove your theory of heredity?

In these experiments [19] it was found that rats with enriched experience, as compared with animals kept in isolation, showed an increase in weight of units of the cortex, an increase in thickness and in acetylcholinesterase activity (an indicator of physiological activity of nervous tissue). The differences were all small—on the order of 5%. Vint's differences between Negroes and Whites were on the order of 15%.

18. A Report from the National Scholarship Service and Fund for Negro Students, *New York Times*, Dec. 12, 1963.
19. *Science*, Oct. 30, 1964, 146: pp. 610-619.

The experimenters used a "bright" strain and a "dull" strain of rats. In the tests the bright strain showed larger effects in all measurements than the dull strain. Also several times greater differences in cholinesterase activity were produced by breeding than were produced by differential experience.

In other words these experiments tend to support my position rather than to contradict it. Consider your own body. You know that your physical structure can be modified *within limits* by physical exercise and by heavy or spare eating. But you cannot eat or exercise yourself into the body of a world champion weight lifter. The fundamentals are controlled by heredity.

I do not believe any scientist today would deny that somewhat the same principles may apply to the brain. The details cannot be considered settled, but it is safe to state that you will never think yourself into the brain of an Einstein. Most significant of all, of course, is the fact that the bright strain of rats showed greater response to improved environment than the dull. If we applied these results to our own race problem it would simply serve to illustrate further that improved environment, equally applied, increases race differences instead of lessening them.

According to the genetic evidence you provided on the difference between the average Negro and the average White, similar differences should exist between intra-marrying populations within the white race. Do you believe that such differences exist between the white populations in the civilized world? And if you do, who are the superior and who are the inferior?

Let me repeat, the differences between averages among the substocks of the White race are *not* similar to the differences between the White race and the Negro.[20]

I will not attempt to rank populations within the Caucasian race as to specific traits except to say that when it comes to the faculty for maintaining stable, free societies I believe that the substock

---

20. It is of course possible to make comparisons between substandard groups and above-standard groups among White substocks and develop differences equal to White-Negro differences, but not between substock averages.

amalgam usually referred to as the English-speaking peoples holds the championship.

What possible pertinency to the question under discussion (that of the American Negro in American society) may be inferred from the Congo situation?

If one wants to study the properties of a substance one seeks as undiluted a sample as possible. The Congo Negro is a fair sample of the West African Negro stocks from which our Negroes are derived.

PSYCHOLOGY

a. *It is an established fact that in World War II the over-all average I.Q. score was higher for the Northern Negro than the Southern White. Since this average was based on all those drafted (rather than the top and bottom), how do you explain this in terms other than environment? If environment is accepted, does this not also apply to the Negro situation?*

b. *Don't you believe that motivation has much to do with the achievement of the Negro? i.e., that the Negro does not see the reason for education since he does not have the opportunity to practice his skills. Also in this line how would you explain the fact (I'll be happy to cite) that Negro children have a higher aspirational level than White children?*

a. There was no such thing as an "I.Q. score" in World War II. If you are talking about the Army General Classification Test, you have your facts reversed. The Southern White excelled the Northern Negro on this test. Five times as many Southern Whites as Northern Negroes, per capita, were in Grade I.[21]

b. Negroes have very high aspirations, often based on envy, but these are not matched by their performance. It is because of their high aspirational level that Negroes want the short cuts which they are unable to create themselves. The Jews, and many others, have found added motivation in hardship and persecution.

---

21. Shuey, p. 352.

Are you aware of the conclusions published by a University of Chicago team of M.D.'s, psychologists and educators (e.g., Atlantic Monthly, 1963) which clearly demonstrate the fact that the I.Q. shifts upward over 40 points in most cases when the poor climate for education is changed to a better one?

You apparently are referring to Murray Friedman's article in the January, 1963, *Atlantic*. While I find nothing in it about 40 I.Q. points, it does speak of "dramatic success achieved in raising I.Q.'s" and thus presents a question I would like to clarify.

There is much discussion today about just what an I.Q. test is intended to measure, and how far it accomplishes its purpose. I believe I state the classical view correctly when I say that ideally an I.Q. test is supposed to determine the intellectual potential of the mind—the raw or virgin brain power—divorced as much as possible from environmental factors. But no test can be given in a vacuum, some words and symbols have to be used, and the moment these are introduced environmental factors do creep in. All we can say is that the test is intended as far as possible to reduce their influence.

Theoretically, and in the ideal sense, an I.Q. score should change only to the extent that exercise of a capacity increases that capacity within the limits of innate potential. Actually an I.Q. score is made up of innate potential, plus practice, plus past experience in varying degrees. I would say that a test which showed a shift of 40 points was either not intended as a genuine I.Q. test or was poorly administered in the first instance.

If an individual is ill or scared or given a test completely alien to his experience, large changes might occur. However, the Negro child gets around quite a bit these days, more in some respects than the White child, and the terms and symbols used in Negro testing should not significantly handicap him in a properly ad-ministered test. What you have in the case you mention is prob-ably less an improvement in I.Q. than in the tools with which the individual expressed his I.Q. Education is such a tool.

Here again we must face the fact that when you give two groups of different potential the same education you do not decrease the gap between them. You increase it, because the group with the higher potential will derive more from the education. Since no one has yet proposed that White environment be held constant while Negro environment is advanced, environmental improvement will only intensify the problem of race differences.

How can your assume any validity in I.Q. tests when those tests have been standardized exclusively from White populations?

The American Negro speaks English, has grown up in an American culture and should experience no handicap in taking "White tests." The Japanese in California don't. Moreover, the Negro must live in our White society. What we are trying to measure is his ability to adapt to our society and to contribute to it. To the extent that the Negro does experience difficulty in taking White tests to just that extent will the nature of his mind be alien to the White mind. We have a culture based on abstract thought. The Negro is poor at abstract thinking. If this shows up in a test it does not invalidate the test. It confirms its validity.

Would you comment on the superiority of the Jewish Race (via your I.Q. reasoning)?

Jews, who are not a race but a substock of the Caucasian race, test as well or better than American non-Jews on "verbal" tests, somewhat below on manipulative tests. The traits which have led to the persecution of Jews have had nothing to do with their intelligence.

The Negro population of the United States is only ten per cent of the White. Many of these Negroes have White genes. What possible difference could so small a mixture make to the country as a whole?

In the first place the ratio of Negro to White is much higher than ten per cent in the South. It ranges up to a majority in some counties, besides which there are relatively few White genes in Deep South Negroes as you can see by observation.

Secondly, and of greater importance, Sir Julian Huxley has estimated [22] that a decrease of one and one-half per cent in the

---

22. Sir Julian Huxley. "Eugenics in Evolutionary Perspective," 1963,

average I.Q. of large groups decreases by 50 per cent the number
of those with an I.Q. of 160 or higher. If my arithmetic is correct, and remembering we have already allowed for the White
genes in American Negroes in the 20 point I.Q. difference, then
we can take ten per cent of 20 points and get 2 points as the
national I.Q. drop from absorption of the Negro. This is larger
than Huxley's one and one-half per cent, and would produce
more than a 50 per cent drop in the over-160 I.Q. group. It
might well be a 70 per cent drop.

Since a civilization is totally dependent for leadership upon a
thin top layer of its population, it is obvious that such a decline
would be disastrous for the United States.

*You say the evidence shows as environment improves, per-
formance doesn't improve. Have you read some contrary evidence
and, if so, how do you refute it?*

It depends whether you are speaking of intelligence or character. Any environment improves intellectual and physical performance when it allows for a better expression of one's abilities—it
does not create abilities. Practice improves a man's golf but only
so far as his innate capacity permits. Practice alone will never
make an Arnold Palmer.

Crime and immorality are in a somewhat different category.
I have not attempted a detailed study of the national figures, but
it is common knowledge that the Negro is pushing forward faster
today than ever before [23] and more efforts are being made to encourage him, yet his relative crime and illegitimacy rates are increasing. The FBI will confirm this to you.

a. *You made reference to a survey in which Negroes and Caucasians coming from similar social and economic backgrounds
took an I.Q. test in which the Negroes made consistently lower
scores than the Whites. Is it your opinion, then, that Negroes possessing lower I.Q.'s can produce the same social and economic*

Perspectives in Biology and Medicine, Vol. VI, No. 2, pp. 165-6.
    23. For a recent survey of Negro advances, see *U.S. News and World
Report,* Dec. 13, 1965, pp. 68-72.

level of living as that of the Whites who have higher I.Q.'s?

b. *You compared the Negro's situation to that of a minor whose adult rights are curtailed because the average minor is not capable of using these rights properly. However, society has taken it upon itself to compensate the minor economically because of his inferior status—that is, the legal guardian or the state is legally required to support the minor until he reaches majority. Do you feel that if the Negroes' status is inferior, the government should compensate it economically?*

a. Equal socio-economic backgrounds are not necessarily the result of, nor do they produce, equal I.Q.'s. They do, however, remove the argument that environment is suppressing the I.Q.

b. Because an analogy is used to illustrate one facet of a situation does not mean that it applies to all other facets of the situation, nor do I believe it to be the duty of intelligent people (through the "State") to provide unintelligent people with the same standard of living as themselves. Exceptionally strong women who, because of the limitations of the average woman, are forbidden to work overtime in factories, are not compensated by the state. Neither is the average woman.

The essence of your argument seems to be that integration in "genetic" situations would tend to decrease the standard deviation of potentialities, i.e., sacrifice exceptional individuals to decrease the percentage of substandard individuals, whereas the accumulated evidence supports the view that marital selection through social channels has tended to increase the standard deviation, i.e., increase the variability of potentials. Would you comment on this?

I have seen no evidence, accumulated or isolated, that indiscriminate marriage (which is what you end up with after total integration has operated for a few generations under the pressures of an equalitarian ideology) increases the deviation at the upper end of the scale. In fact, all the evidence is to the contrary. This is what a civilization must be most concerned about. Do you for one moment contend that the amalgamation of two groups, one with an I.Q. 15 or 20 points below the other, is not going to result in a mean I.Q. below that of the higher group?

Do you feel that tests evaluating Negro intelligence are scientifically justifiable even though contemporary society has impressed upon the Negro his innate inferiority? How can you free the Negro from the stigma of inferiority so that an honest evaluation of his intelligence can be made?

Contemporary society has impressed upon me the fact that I am not a fit bridge partner for Charles Goren. Does this lower my playing performance within my own capacity?

If "anyone's position can be improved by education," why not simply educate Negroes—it seems you have invalidated your own argument. About Brown vs. Board of Education—state your sources on "new evidence"—were these from Southern courts?

I have never suggested that Negroes not be educated. I suggest Whites be educated, too, and when both groups are educated the gap between them is simply increased, for the reason that the capacity of the White to receive education is greater than the Negro's.

As to *Brown vs. Board of Education,* evidence never comes from courts; it comes from witnesses. The chief witness in the *Brown* case was a Negro. The witnesses in *Stell* and *Evers* were from both North and South. If you want to read the evidence you can do so by ordering the transcript in any of these cases (at considerable cost) from George Leonard, 1730 K St., N.W., Washington, D. C. 20006, or you can write for the opinions and findings of fact of the judges (at modest cost), also from Mr. Leonard.

How do you account for the so-called "exceptional" Negro? Is he the result of a genetic mutation; or perhaps the result of being fortunate enough to realize his actual potential despite people like you?

Variability will account for the exceptional Negro, a factor which is supplemented in many areas and most cases by some

White ancestry. In a study of bright Negroes done in Chicago, 80 per cent reported some White ancestry.[24]

If environment plays virtually no role in aiding the intelligence of a person, then why were the Negroes from Northern states able to score better than Whites from the South during World War I? Didn't you admit education was a factor in this case?

I did not say environment played "virtually no role." I said it played a minor role—about one-quarter, to be specific. I also explained the reason for the World War I results, namely, first, the best of the Negroes were compared with the worst of the Whites and, second, the test used was not for I.Q. but was one which reflected educational experience.

Certainly education is a factor. Even an animal's performance can be improved by education, up to the limits of its innate capacity.

If we assume your facts to be correct, what does a democratic society care about intermarriage, etc., of different I.Q. groups, etc.?

A democratic society ought to care about the qualities in its population which have made it capable of becoming and maintaining a stable, free civilization. No Negro population has ever been able to do this, for reasons which I have already examined; therefore, to the extent that a successful free society absorbs a Negro population, to that same extent will its success decline.

Even accepting your assertion of racial differences, if there is a significant overlap should not divisions in classes in schools be made on the basis of individual ability instead of race, putting the superior Negro with the superior Whites?

I have already quoted at some length from the federal court's findings on this point in the *Stell* case. Now let me give you what a federal court in another case had to say on the same subject. Here are the findings of the judge in *Evers:*

24. Paul Witty, "Research on the American Negro," 1940, *39th Year Book, National Society for the Study of Education*, pp. 261-9.

"The differences so measured [between White and Negro children] were not limited to the change of learning rate and ultimate difference in relative mental age or I.Q. which the Court has previously noted, but included as well an even more fundamental distinction in educational patterns, that of subject interest and problem approach. The witnesses were unanimous that these differences were not only substantial in themselves but were of major importance in determining the method of teaching, the selection and content of courses and fixing the progress norms. This was true even though an individual of one group would overlap the other in one or more of the measured factors since these did not show a change in the over-all pattern."

In other words, educability is a matter of more than I.Q., and overlap in I.Q. does not necessarily mean overlap in other important factors. I might go further and point out that there is no such thing as "overlap" except in a specific quality. Educability is the learning pattern of an individual taken in totality and is made up of hundreds of traits. Overlap in all of these traits would simply mean that a child was not a Negro. To force Negro and White children into schools together may result in injury to the brighter Negro child as great as, or greater than, the injury to the average Negro.

Speaking of *Evers,* I would like to quote you another comment of the court in that case which has a bearing on your question:

"Apart from any differences in learning aptitude between white and Negro pupils, the evidence showed without contradiction that effective learning can only occur under conditions in which the individual's attention can be given to study without unnatural distractions. Such receptivity occurs only when the learner is in a group with which he has an empathic relation, such as with his family, his kind, his neighbors of like interests, or other groups with which he identifies himself as an individual and in which, because of his similarity of characteristic, he is an accepted group member."

All of the evidence in *Stell, Evers* and the companion cases [25]

25. *Davis vs. Board of School Commissioners of Mobile County, Ala.,* 219 F. Supp. 542 (S.D. Ala. 1963); *Armstrong vs. Board of Education of City of Birmingham, Ala.,* 220 F. Supp. 217 (N.D. Ala. 1963); *Gibson vs.*

points up a fact which the Supreme Court did not consider in *Brown,* namely, that there is a basic human need for self-identification with one's own kind which is part of the healthy psychological development of every individual. The Court in *Evers* continued:

"It does not appear that this identification is caused either by school or society but rather arises primarily from a natural biological selection mechanism which plays a part in maintaining evolutionary diversity of type and is described scientifically as ethnocentrism. While race preferences resulting from gross race differences may be consciously overridden by mature individuals, they remain as an inherent mechanism so that no individual ever becomes completely unconscious of such a difference.

"In the classroom, the intermingling of two groups, each having a high degree of self-identity, causes a heightening of consciousness of group, a result which grows as the number of contacts between them is increased. Compulsory intermixing therefore exaggerates rather than diminishes any divisive forces which exist."

One of the more pathetic sights to be witnessed in schools with token, or "bright Negro pupil," integration nowadays is the isolation of the solitary Negro in the classroom and of his family at school functions. There is, of course, the embarrassed effort to make every one seem at home, there are forced smiles and synthetic gaiety as attempts are launched to digest the indigestible. But the folly on both sides, and the cruelty to the Negro child, must make the informed observer wince.

I doubt this would have been the case had progress continued along pre-1954 lines. All the uproar and justifiable opposition which follows in the wake of what is now called the Negro "revolution" have only focussed a spotlight on the exceptional Negro and made him a symbol of the compulsory integration movement. Indeed, the Negro on the light side of the spectrum, the mulatto, is always the one with the hardest problem, and the one whose occasional presence, under the old dispensation, would quietly have come to be accepted.

Glynn County Board of Education, U.S.D.C. Southern District of Georgia, Brunswick Division (1963). (Unreported.)

In what state did the Evers trial take place?

Are the actions of Black Congolese Rebels to be considered any more condemnable than the actions of White Germans under Hitler?

The *Evers* trial took place in Mississippi. If it had taken place in North Dakota and the decision had been different, would a Southerner be correct in accusing the Northern Court of prejudice?

The difference between the Congo and Germany under Hitler is that the behavior of the rebels in the Congo is standard procedure when the Negro is left to his own devices under similar circumstances, whereas the behavior of the Germans under Hitler was an exception to the rule among White men.

Moreover, the civilized free world combined against Hitler. The civilized free world today, befuddled by a socialist-motivated scientific fraud, is not only not combining against the atrocities in Africa—by withdrawing its controls, it is actually encouraging them.

How do you explain the fact that not one member of the National Education Association or the American Federation of Teachers has endorsed your belief that integration is bad (in the classroom situation) and that the NEA has stated positively that integration has no bad effect? (Fact citation can be found in NEA Journal.)

The NEA is part of the educational establishment whose motivations I have already examined. The record in *Stell* and *Evers,* and other companion cases, is replete with study after study on the adverse effect of integration. These were sponsored by scientific witnesses under oath and subject to cross-examination. No members of the associations you mention ventured to appear.

Why do Negro children score higher on I.Q. tests when the test is administered by Negro testers? This holds true especially on Achievement Tests.

Your facts have been disputed, but even if they are correct, what difference does it make? White children still do better than Negroes even when the latter are tested by Negroes. All that your point seems to prove is that Negroes are more relaxed and accomplish more in the presence of other Negroes, which is a good reason for Negro teachers and classmates.

If you were to take two 400-lb. alligators—one with a brain weight of 17 g. and the other with a brain weight of 13 g.—and the latter were transported to a zoo and conditioned to certain responses, would you then assume that alligators with a brain weight of 13 g.—as an average, of course—have a greater intelligence? Thus, are you saying that brain weight is proportionate to intelligence? Is the size of the brain relative to intelligence?

You are mixing several factors in this question. First, I have already explained that an I.Q., properly determined, is not radically changed by education, although I have qualified this by adding that education will always improve performance up to the limits of innate capacity. Second, I have emphasized that brain weight or size is only part of the story concerning intelligence in any individual case—cortex area, proportion of parts and cyto-architecture are also involved. I leave you to apply these variables to your alligators.

If you use inferior brain potential as justification for segregation would this apply to Caucasians with damaged or slightly retarded brains as well?

By definition, damaged or slightly retarded brains are not a group characteristic of Caucasians, whereas a lower I.Q. and other differences *are* group characteristics of Negroes. Obviously if brain damage or retardation is significant such individual Caucasians are segregated.

You admit that the difficulty with integration is that it leads inevitably to intermarriage and this in turn would lead to abasement of the genetic stock and a degeneration of the general level of intelligence. This would occur because the frequency of high intelligence in Negroes is significantly less than in Whites. You also admit that in some cases Negroes equal or excel some Whites in intelligence. Interbreeding of these Negroes with Whites would

*not necessarily debase the genetic stock and in some cases might
even raise the level. If we may ignore the practical difficulties a
moment, should you not in consistency be advocating segregation
of the intelligent from the less gifted regardless of race—since
intelligence is the issue you find important?*

I have already answered this question from several angles but
I will summarize: First, educability is not solely a matter of
intelligence. It involves subject interest and problem approach
which have been found to differ between Whites and Negroes
among the exceptional as well as the average. Second, we cannot
ignore the practical difficulties—organizing a society is a practical
matter. Consider my references to exceptional minors and women.
Third, once the doors of White society are thrown open to exceptional Negroes in those areas where mates are chosen it would
be virtually impossible to close them in the face of other Negroes
because of the ideological pressures of the equalitarian movement. Fourth, race mixture involves not only intelligence levels,
but also temperament, degrees of courage or lack of it, character,
and so on, as well as physical differences which may create organic
disharmony in a crossing. Fifth, your suggestion is academic
because the Supreme Court's 1954 decision and the Civil Rights
Act require indiscriminate integration.

*How could you ask for a finer public servant than Edward
Brooke, the Senator from Massachusetts? He disproves your theory
of inferiority.*

Look at Edward Brooke's face. Do you consider him a typical
Negro? And if you do not, why do you use him as an argument?
Can you not see that in doing so you are misleading the unin-
formed as to what the real issues are?

In any large community there are Negro men to admire and
Negro women who are equally fine. From observation I would
judge there is as much overlap in character and charm as there
is in intelligence, although here again it usually seems related to
some white blood. I touched on this problem in considerable
detail in the last chapter of *Race and Reason* and will not repeat
myself here.

a. *100 years ago how many Negroes could top White men in I.Q. tests and how many Negroes can now? That is: has not the Negro improved slightly under segregation and greatly under integration, and none in slavery?*

b. *Why can't a culture be adopted?*

a. The Negro has improved greatly under segregation; it is not apparent that he has done as well under the limited integration he has experienced.[26]

b. Because a culture is the product of the innate capacity of the race which created it. It can to some extent be parasitically enjoyed by races of less capacity, but it can neither be advanced nor independently sustained by such races.

Since the Orientals in our society have a much lower crime rate and illegitimacy than the average White in our society, and since differences between peoples are genetic in origin by a 3 to 1 ratio—can it not therefore be inferred that the Oriental is indeed not only the Caucasian's equal, but his superior?

In some respects quite possibly. I cannot verify your figures as I have not studied them. I have stated previously that the English speaking stocks of the Caucasian race probably hold the championship in maintaining stable, free societies.

You stated that the lack of perfect evidence of the Negro's inequality (inferiority) is no reason to assume that he is equal. Is it not equally true that imperfect evidence of his equality is no reason to assume he is inferior. Particularly since, contrary to your assertion, the balance of evidence does indicate that the Negro is potentially equal, but lacking the social and cultural advantages.

Your facts are wrong. You assume that the evidence is equal, in amount and in imperfection, on each side. The truth of the matter is that the evidence is overwhelming on the side of inequality—indeed I know of no evidence at all on the side of equality. What I said was that because *every item* of the evidence

26. See *supra,* p. 113.

for inequality was not perfect was no reason for assuming that the opposite of the evidence was true.

When your group of scientists say one thing, and we are taught that a much larger group of scientists say something else, how are we to decide which is correct except by the preponderance of opinion?

By learning to think for yourselves, which is one of the chief objects of education. In this case it is not a difficult task. All you need to do is to stop taking unsupported assertions as final and demand to look at the evidence. There will soon be no question left in your mind.

CIVIL RIGHTS

Is not the right to integrate a constitutional right?

There is no "right" to integration, either in our Constitution, our moral code, or our religious precepts. Segregation *for valid reasons* is an accepted social procedure. I cannot claim that I am denied "equal rights" or "civil rights" as an American, or that I am made a second-class citizen, or that I am deprived of "human dignity", if I am refused the use of a ladies' rest room or if, having a contagious disease, I am placed in a segregated hospital. We need be concerned only with whether the reasons for segregating the Negro are valid, and this is where the question of the genetic versus the environmental source of his limitations becomes decisive.

The Negro's so-called "constitutional" right to integration derives solely from the Supreme Court's decision in the *Brown* case. As we have seen, this case was based upon misrepresentation and concealment of vital evidence bearing upon the genetic issue.

You often speak of segregation in "social" situations. What do you mean by a "social" situation?

Any situation which has genetic implications. These are the situations which produce instinctive tensions, and logical tensions as well, because they invite the possibility of interbreeding. But when it comes to deciding what is or is not a social situation we are confronted with great local variations. A restaurant in a small Mississippi town may be very different in this respect from a restaurant at the Grand Central Station in New York. The same may be true of other forms of public accommodations, or indeed any aspect of community life.

I do not suppose we have ever faced a situation where the advantages of the dispersive aspects of our federal system as originally designed could be more wisely applied, and are being more callously disregarded. There are many areas of the North and West with relatively minor Negro populations in which policies entirely different from those in areas with large Negro populations would be justified.

They have a rule of thumb in the South that the Negro problem does not become serious until the ratio approaches ten to fifteen per cent, but regardless of this flash point, when one considers the spectrum nature of the race problem—the shift in this spectrum toward the mulatto in certain Northern areas a swell as the variability in the quantity of Negroes—it is folly to attempt to deal with it by one set of laws or customs everywhere.

I cannot over-emphasize the importance of the concept of variability in dealing with any racial problem. We have the variability of the genetic spectrum, of the population ratio, and finally of the community setting. Consider a small town in Montana which has two or three Negro families whose predominantly White genes show in blue eyes, straight hair, sharp noses, and relatively high I.Q., and whose Negro genes are only apparent in skin color; then compare this town with one in Alabama where the population is over fifty per cent Negro of pure or nearly pure blood, with prognathous jaws, kinky hair, flat noses, everted lips and relatively low I.Q. In the first situation it might be justifiable to have no segregation at all, while in the second some segregation might be essential.

What could be more apt to invite community disruption than to try to control racial problems in those two towns by the same set of laws made by politicians sitting in Washington and hoping to win the Negro vote in New York—or by a Supreme Court which has heard only one side of the evidence on genetic racial differences?

But should not everyone be equal at least before the law?

Before the law, yes, but this does not mean that the law should be everywhere the same. Circumstances alter cases. We find a great variation in laws throughout the United States. Consider the liquor laws or the speed laws. Some communities prefer certain things one way, some another. It is when the federal government steps in to force the views of one section upon another whose circumstances are different that trouble starts.

What about voting? Surely here the law should be identical everywhere?

It would undoubtedly be unreasonable to say that simply because a man is a Negro he cannot vote, but on the other hand it may be essential as a practical matter to establish a more rigorous procedure for selection of voters, both white and black, in communities with heavy Negro concentrations since the consequences of a failure in, or evasion of, the procedure are more serious.

We know, for example, that Negroes as a race have never been able to maintain a stable, free society, anywhere, any time—in fact, government by a Negro majority invariably results in chaos. We may even question whether, based on historical experience, the average Negro really prefers a republic to other forms of government. His standards of fiscal responsibility are quite different from the White. Our own American experience has proven that his vote is more easily bought and that he is more apt to vote as a bloc. With large numbers of Negroes in a community, therefore, it is vital to be *sure* that the level of intelligence of the voting Negro is high, even if this means cutting out larger numbers of less intelligent Whites than might be necessary in an all White community.

One of the more alarming things to me about the current political scene is the blindness and stupidity of the politician who openly seeks, and brags of capturing, the Negro vote—meaning the vote of the average Negro. This is the equivalent of saying:

"My policies have attracted the approval of a race, the degree of whose participation in public affairs has always been a measure of the deterioration of the society in which it occurs."

I am indebted to the government of Rhodesia for the following summary of the manner in which the problem is handled there. While the situation is different from that in the southern United States, the method has some thought-provoking aspects:

"The franchise is for voters of all races registered on one of two rolls and extends to all citizens aged 21 years or over, resident in the country for more than two years, subject to certain property, income or educational qualifications. Of the Legislative Assembly of 65 members, 50 are elected to represent constituencies by the more highly qualified voters of the 'A' roll, whilst 15, representing electoral districts, are elected by the voters with lower qualifications on the 'B' roll. Both constituencies and electoral districts cover the entire country and the decision as to which roll a person qualifies for, or stands for Parliament on, is in no way dependent on race.

" 'A' Roll: (a) Income of £792 or ownership of property of value of £1,650; or (b) Income of £528 or ownership of property of value of £1,100 AND completion of a course of primary education; or (c) Income of £330 or ownership of property of value of £550 AND four years' secondary education; or (d) Appointment to the office of Chief or Headman.

" 'B' Roll: (a) Income of £264 or ownership of property of the value of £495; or (b) Income of £132 or ownership of property of the value of £275 AND two years' secondary education; or (c) Over 30 years of age AND income of £132 or ownership of property of value of £275 AND primary education; or (d) Over 30 years of age AND income of £198 or ownership of property of value of £385; or (e) Kraal heads with a following of 20 or more heads of families; or (f) Ministers or religion.

"There is no legal impediment to a Rhodesian of any race becoming Prime Minister, Member of Parliament, Judge of the High Court, Head of a Government Department or practicing in any profession.

Commenting upon the above suffrage requirements the Rhodesian Minister of Information writes:

"Without the establishment of men trained in and accustomed to the art of government, men accustomed to ensuring order and obedience to order, which is indispensable to progress, happiness and human civilization, any society must relapse into anarchy or become an absolute dictatorship.

"It is this basic fact that is at the root of our Rhodesian philosophy, which is that a country is amply justified in limiting the franchise to those of its inhabitants capable of exercising it with reason, judgment and public spirit.

"We seek to ensure this by two means—firstly an educational test on the theory that you thereby have a mind that is trained and disciplined in some degree, and secondly, a means test on the theory that a man earning more than a mere subsistence or acquiring property of some substance has the necessary qualities of character and mind.

"There can be no general rule without hard cases, but no one has yet devised a more certain, practical or logical approach to the exercise of the franchise. What we do know is that there can be no progress on the basis of an uninformed, emotional mass electorate and that adult suffrage, inherent in majority rule would, in Rhodesia, place control in the hands of those unequipped to exercise it. The mob may be able to form judgments of the personal qualities of candidates—but that is not enough, for a voter must be able to form an opinion of the merits of the policy presented to him."

The unlimited suffrage concept is marginal when applied to a homogeneous electorate consisting of an advanced and experienced race like the Anglo-American. To apply it to states or communities with high percentages of a retarded race is suicidal.

Apparently you have no faith in democracy. Are you not attacking the principle of "one man, one vote"?

There has never been any one-man-one-vote principle practiced before in our republic, or in any successful free society, if that is what you mean by "democracy". When Athenian democracy was in its prime, large segments of the population were not allowed to vote. Women were not allowed to vote in the United States when I was a boy, and they are not allowed to vote on federal issues in Switzerland today. Until recently, and under our Constitution as it has hitherto been interpreted, the qualifiication of voters has been left exclusively to the states, except that by constitutional amendment (1870) Negroes as such cannot be discriminated against by state laws, and women were given the vote in 1920.

It is time Americans remembered that when Daniel Webster called our government the last, best hope of earth he was referring to a representative constitutional republic, the special genius of which was the way in which the top was protected from exploitation by the bottom and vice versa. There were all sorts of provisions by which this balance was assured, many of which have been whittled away, and always in favor of the bottom. If this keeps up, it can only end in the collapse of the "the last, best hope" because it will mean injustice, and injustice to either the top or bottom will produce rebellion and violence in the long run. Exclusive victory for the top means fascism, for the bottom, communism.

What about jurors?
I feel the same way about jury duty as about voting.

Do not all your qualifications concerning treatment of the Negro result in limiting his equality of opportunity?
In the majority of cases the Negro's failure is not due to a lack of opportunity but to a lack of capability. It is always easy to blame the latter on the former because opportunity itself is not easy to define. Two runners with unequal strength do not have an equal opportunity to win a race. Must we, nevertheless, allow all runners to enter every race regardless of past performance? Must every tennis player in the world be allowed to enter the U.S. National Championships each September? Obviously this is impossible.

In the case of Negroes in general it is only natural that judgments should be made upon average past performance and the individual Negro regarded with some skepticism. For this reason there may be some opportunities that even the exceptional Negro is denied but these are relatively rare. Most Negroes with intelligence and character have made their way very well in the United States.[27]

___

27. See, for example, the case of S. B. Fuller, Negro president of the

You refer to Abraham Lincoln's segregationist attitudes: in his day, these attitudes were liberal beyond belief. Should our society remain so static that what was a valid idea a hundred years ago remains unchanged today? Would Lincoln express these same beliefs today?

In his day Lincoln was *not* liberal beyond belief. It was the Northern abolitionists who were the fanatical liberals of the time. To Lincoln not slavery but secession was the issue in the Civil War.

Apparently you assume that in order not to remain static a society must move in the direction of equalitarian socialism, which is first cousin to communism. I do not agree with you. I believe such movement is deterioration, not progress.

How about references on Abe Lincoln?

The most cited reference on Lincoln is from his speech at Charleston, Illinois, in September 1858 when he was debating with Douglas. (See any collection of these debates.) In this speech he said "I am not, nor ever have been, in favor of bringing about in any way the social and political equality of the white and black races; I am not, nor ever have been, in favor of making voters or jurors of Negroes, nor qualifying them to hold office."

However, in view of the distortions in the press concerning Lincoln's views on the Negro which always appear around Lincoln's birthday, I believe it will be helpful to quote in part a letter written to the *Washington Post* on March 3, 1964 by Ludwell H.

Fuller Products Company, Chicago. His organization contains 10 subsidiaries in 38 states, maintains 80 branch offices and employs more than 5,000 people. In addition, Fuller is publisher of *The Courier* chain of national weekly newspapers, director of a bank and member of the Board of the Chicago Association of Commerce and Industry. In a recent speech he said: "It is contrary to the laws of nature for man to stand still; he must move forward or the eternal march of progress will force him backward. This the Negro has failed to understand; he believes that the lack of civil rights legislation, and the lack of integration have kept him back. But this is not true; the lack of initiative, courage, integrity, loyalty and wisdom are responsible for his not making the rate of progress that he should make." Speech before the National Association of Manufacturers, *New York Herald Tribune*, Dec. 7, 1963.

Johnson, Associate Professor of History at William and Mary College. It is the most impartial summary of the matter I have seen. The circumstances which gave rise to it are sufficiently explained in its first paragraph:

"I have no connection with any organizations espousing either integration or segregation, but I do have an obligation to historical accuracy. In an editorial of February 10, you commented adversely on an advertisement by the Citizens' Councils of America which quoted from one of the Lincoln-Douglas debates and from some remarks Lincoln made to a Negro delegation in 1862. In those quotations Lincoln expressed himself as being in favor of segregation and Negro colonization. Your editorial remarked that the advertisement 'dishonors the memory of Abraham Lincoln and does injustice to Negro Americans.'

"It is not at all clear to me that the century-old opinions of Lincoln shed any light on contemporary race problems, but since the *Post* editors consented to debate the issue on this level, some attempt should be made to rescue history from the propagandists.

"Anyone contending that Lincoln was in favor of Negro equality must assume the burden of proof. The evidence you present consists of two quotations. In the first Lincoln says: 'I adhere to the Declaration of Independence. If Judge Douglas and his friends are not willing to stand by it, let them come up and amend it. Let them make it read that all men are created equal except negroes.' This you propose to 'fling into the face of the Citizens' Council of America.' In that *same* speech Lincoln said: 'I also yield to all which follows from that necessity [the presence of the Negro]. What I would most desire would be the separation of the white and black races.' Will you also fling *that* in the faces of the Citizens' Council? Your animadversions about quotations taken out of context thus seem somewhat unbecoming. The plain fact is, as even the most cursory examination of the 1858 debates will show, that Lincoln repeatedly stated his belief that the Declaration applied to Negroes and also that he was in favor of white supremacy—often in the same speeches.

"No one can deny that Lincoln was opposed to slavery. But his position on the race question is altogether a different matter. During the 1850's, and especially during the debates with Douglas, Lincoln stated unequivocally that he was opposed to: (1) the state of Illinois bestowing citizenship on its Negroes; (2) enfranchising Negroes; (3) allowing them to serve on juries; (4) social equality. One of the reasons he gave for opposing territorial slavery was a desire to preserve the West for free white men. Furthermore, he was a long-time advocate of colonization in the tradition of Henry Clay, whom he so greatly admired. In 1854, for example, Lincoln said that his first impulse as to the method of dealing with slavery would be to free the slaves and send them to Liberia, although he saw grave difficulties in the way. In 1857 he was more hopeful, saying: 'The enterprise is a difficult one; but "when there is a will there is a way"; and what colonization needs most is a hearty will.' As President he attempted with remarkable persistency (even after the Emancipation Proclamation) to carry out this project. In his first annual message to Congress he asked for money to finance colonization, saying: 'On this whole proposition, including the appropriation of money with the acquisition of territory, does not the expediency amount to absolute necessity—that without which the Government itself cannot be perpetuated?' In his second annual message in December 1862, Lincoln asked for a constitutional amendment that would allow Congress to appropriate money for colonization. In 1863 a colony was actually established on Ile a Vache, Haiti, but it was a dismal failure, and the survivors were brought back the following year. In July, 1864, Lincoln's private secretary, John Hay, noted in his diary that the President had finally given up colonization.

"Back in 1854, Lincoln had said, suppose colonization proved to be impracticable — 'What then? Free them all, and keep them among us as underlings? Is it quite certain that this betters their condition? I think I would not hold one in slavery, at any rate; yet the point is not clear enough for me to denounce people upon. What next? Free them, and make them politically and socially our equals? My own feelings will not admit of this; and if mine would, we well know that those of the great mass of white people will not.'

"The most advanced position Lincoln ever took as to the rights of Negroes was in a letter of March 13, 1864, in which he wrote to the Union governor of Louisiana to 'barely suggest for your private consideration' that those Negroes who were 'very intelligent' or who had fought in the Union army be allowed to vote in state elections; but this was, Lincoln concluded, 'only a suggestion.' Lincoln, like Jefferson and unlike the doctrinaire integrationist of today, realized the profound complexity of the race question and believed, again like Jefferson, that the only sure solution was colonization. . . .

"The other piece of evidence you present in rebuttal, a quotation from a letter Lincoln is supposed to have written early in

1864, saying that 'the restoration of the Union must rest upon the principle of civil and political equality of both races,' is of doubtful authenticity, in spite of its inclusion in the most recent collection of Lincoln's works. This purported letter was printed in the *New York Tribune* on September 26, 1865, in the midst of the developing controversy over Reconstruction policies. The source given by the *Tribune* was the *Southern Advocate,* a paper which has never come to light, let alone the original letter. On the face of it it appears unlikely that Lincoln would have made such a statement at the same time he was trying to induce Negroes to leave the country altogether . . ."

This should be the letter to end all letters on Lincoln and the Negro. The claims by Republican liberals at the 1964 Republican Convention that they represented the Lincoln Wing of the party are among the more fanciful fabrications of our time.

For the sake of this question, I will grant you the validity of your "facts." If you can show the average brain capacity of a group of black, green, purple, or white people less than that of a group of black, green, purple or white group—I say "good for you." It seems that you go on to assert that one should enter into social interaction only with those people of at least equal mental capacity. How, I ask, does one determine an individual's mental capacity, briefly, when meeting him on the street and faced with the momentous decision of whether to accept him as a social equal, or not? I claim that this would be an absurd undertaking, and your assertions are a mere façade for self-righteousness.

Your question involves voluntary social acceptance which is not at issue in this controversy. The purpose of the Negro movement and the practical result of the Supreme Court's decision on schools is to force social acceptance, either directly or by erosion through an ideological fraud equivalent to compulsion. You can do what you please on the street, but there are many people who are going to resent your telling them that they must put their children in schools with Negroes.

Does your concept of Equality suggest that the murderers of Evers, Herbert Lee, Louis Allen, Channey, Schwerner and Good-

man not be brought to justice? Is it because Negroes being inferior must get inferior justice?

Obviously not. Justice should be universal and should prevail in Mississippi. But I will point out that when you force upon 30 million people laws which they know to be destructive of their civilization you are going to increase crime among the more violent elements of the population. The same thing would happen in the North if something equally destructive were forced upon them against *their* convictions.

Your whole speech appears to be more an apology for segregation than a scientific dissertation. You know that segregation has been the cause of lynching, bombing, shooting, beating, unjust jailing in Mississippi. How do you justify this? If we accept segregation on your thesis, we must also justify these things.

Your facts are wrong and your conclusion is a non-sequitur. Segregation has not been the cause of the crimes you mention; the cause has been the attempt at forced integration. To the extent that crimes against the Negro were previously committed by Whites in the South, these were few in comparison to those committed by the Negro against other Negroes. Thousands of Southern communities lived at peace with the Negro before 1954 and some still do.

Aside from genetic considerations, how much do you think segregation has to do with causing the Negro to have such low moral standards, low I.Q., and high rate of illegitimate births and disease?

If a patient has a contagious illness and is segregated from the public, for the public's protection, how much does this have to do with the patient's having the illness?

How do you justify segregation when you know that it is the means of enforcing poverty? 46 per cent of the Negro families in Sunflower County are forced to live on less than $1,000 a year.

Segregation does not enforce poverty. The Jews have frequently been segregated throughout history, but they have not been made poor.

How can you justify discrimination in voting and transportation, for example, on differences in intelligence capacity as the Constitution has no intelligence requirements? Seating in buses is, similarly, not based on I.Q.

The Constitution leaves to the several states the determination of the qualifications for voters, providing only that they be uniformly applied to all races. I have already suggested how this might be done in our South, and have illustrated how it is being done in Rhodesia.

I may remind you, first, that when the Constitution was originally adopted Negroes were chattel property and consequently received no rights thereunder and, second, that when the 14th Amendment was adopted after the Civil War, it was forced upon the South without any pretense of legality. All but one of the Southern States rejected it and it was only ratified by them when, under a law passed by a Congress from which the South had been excluded, they were given no choice save to accept it or submit to military rule. The President vetoed this law, saying that its whole character, scope and object were in palpable conflict with the plainest provisions of the Constitution. The rump Congress over-rode the veto.

However, I am still of the opinion that the Negro can now be held to have many rights under the Constitution and 14th Amendment without the disastrous interpretation placed upon it by the Supreme Court in 1954.

As to transportation, this is not normally a social situation.

You argued with a decision of our Supreme Court. Is not any decision of this Court "The Law of the Land" and not for you to dispute?

Your education has scarcely begun. It is the right of any citizen to disagree with, and lawfully seek to change, any decision of any court. Has it not occurred to you that when the NAACP obtained the decision in *Brown vs. Topeka* (the case on which the integration movement rests) it overthrew the decisions of ninety years? The only difference is that the NAACP obtained this decision by misrepresenting and omitting evidence, while I am trying, as best I can, to restore the original law by telling the truth.

Can you honestly say that segregated facilites in the South are equal? Here is a working example of segregation. Let us look at this.

Segregated schools for Negroes in the South were rapidly being made equal to those of the Whites in physical facilities. This was true long before 1954. Segregated eating places, hotels and stores run by Negroes are usually of low quality. Whose fault is this? Take a long look.

Are not ideas like yours responsible for the terrible way Negroes are treated in South Africa?

Let me answer this question with two of my own: (1) If you had to pick one country in which to live out of the entire African continent, which one would you choose? (2) If Negroes are treated so terribly in South Africa, why is it that 25,000 Negroes manage to enter that country illegally each year and only a few leave?

Today all of the peoples you refer to as backward are demanding their rights and their freedom. The world is in a ferment. It is part of progress. How can you expect to stop it?

Just tell a naïve person often enough that you owe him a living, that he is entitled to share your earnings, that you have cheated him for years, that he has a "right" to your savings and achievements, and watch how quickly he will start to ferment.

The world situation you mention is the product of White socialist indoctrination—of what Churchill called the "gospel of envy." It has no relation to reality. Modern means of transportation and communication have spread this gospel broadcast like a virus. How to stop it except by starting to tell the truth I cannot say. But you may be sure it is no part of "progress".

Governor Scranton suggests that one reason for Goldwater's defeat in the 1964 election was the "exclusive" nature of his appeal to voters—that the Republican party must have a "broader base" and be more attractive to minority groups. Do you agree?

The desirability of exclusiveness depends upon what is excluded. A man who tries to please everybody ends up pleasing nobody, although, if he has enough resources at his disposal, there may be quite a circus for some time.

To please indiscriminately is to do destructive things. To cater to the Negro vote, for example, is to forget that Negro voters, left to themselves, have never been able to operate a free government. When you please the Negro bloc, without carefully examining what you do, you are apt to be injecting into the bloodstream of the body politic the virus of collapse. The body politic in our case may be strong enough to stand a certain amount of such a virus, but it is bound to be weakened by it, and can be destroyed in the long run.

The United States, was founded on, and developed through, the laws, institutions and traditions of the English-speaking stocks of the White race. The majority of our population still consists of these stocks. We will be unwise if we adopt policies to please other stocks or races which either directly violate our institutions or which indirectly, through unrestricted immigration, lead to their violation by so changing the nature of our population that they will be voted or interpreted out of existence.[28]

As a lawyer you should read Prof. Cahn's article "A Dangerous Myth in the School Segregation Cases" [sic] which shows that the Supreme Court did not rely on science in deciding those cases, but just pretended in part to do so out of courtesy to Prof. Clark and his colleagues. The Court decided the cases solely on the grounds that separate but equal schools for Whites and Negroes are inherently unequal and thus violate the 14th Amendment. So all your arguments about science are really beside the point.

---

28. For a further discussion of this subject see *Race and Reason*, p. 104.

Because this article [29] was cited by the Fifth Circuit as its
principal excuse for refusing the plea of the trial court in *Evers*
(they speak of the trial court as "bewitched and bewildered by
the popular myth that *Brown* was decided for sociological reasons
untested in a trial"), I feel justified in making a few frank comments about both the article and the Fifth Circuit.

Cahn's article has two faults. It is misinformed as to the
facts and irrational in handling what facts it has. Cahn begins
by saying that Kenneth Clark with his doll tests was trying to
prove to the Supreme Court what everybody already knew without
his proving it, namely, that a sense of inferiority generated by
segregation damaged the Negro child. He then admitted that
Clark did not do this very well, but that his inadequacies did not
matter, since the Court knew what everybody else knew anyhow.

Cahn was apparently unaware that Clark had conducted earlier
tests on larger numbers of Negro children which flatly contradicted his testimony before the Court and indicated that integration caused greater damage to the Negro child than segregation.
Cahn was also ignorant of the evidence available, but not offered
to the Court, concerning the innate nature of the Negro's limitations—in other words the evidence showing that the "sense of
inferiority" of the Negro was not something initially created by
either segregation or integration, but something due simply to
his biological limitations. The Fifth Circuit knew, or ought to
have known, about these deficiencies in Cahn's article.

It is clear that when you, or Cahn, or a court say that "separate
but equal is inherently unequal" you cannot make the statement
in a vacuum. You must have some justification for it. Vassar
and Yale are separate, but they are not inherently unequal. The
inequality, if such it be, in the case of the separation of Negroes
and Whites can result solely from the implication of inferiority,
which Cahn finds cruel and the Court finds unconstitutional.

Now when evidence exists, but is not introduced at a trial, which
indicates not only that integration increases the sense of inferiority
as compared with segregation, but also that neither segregation

---

29. Edmond Cahn, *Jurisprudence*, 1955, 30 N.Y.U.L. Rev., p. 150.

nor integration creates the inferiority which is due rather to innate limitations and is thus a fact of life, do you, or Cahn, or the Fifth Circuit mean to say that this evidence has no bearing on the issues and that anyone who says it does is bewitched?

Of course the crowning item is the remark by the Fifth Circuit that the appeal of the White children in the *Evers* case "tries the patience of the Court." Let me suggest to the Fifth Circuit that their specious opinions and their lack of moral stamina may someday try the patience of history.

I will also suggest to Prof. Cahn that if he thinks this sort of thing adds to the "dignity and stature of every American" he lacks the Anglo-American concept of what dignity and stature are.

ETHICS

Should we be corrupt and wrong to an individual just for advancement? Should the Negro individual be sacrificed for the White man to avoid "stagnation"?

I have never suggested that we be "corrupt and wrong" to the Negro, or "sacrifice" the Negro. Do we "sacrifice" the individual strong woman when she is not allowed to work overtime in factories, or the individual smart minor when he is not allowed to vote? On the other hand, I see no reason to sacrifice the White race to give the Negro race what it has not earned and does not deserve.

You seem to recognize a certain value in Love. How do you explain in biological and racial terms the White man's apparently inbred or innate propensity to hate Negroes—to lynch and throw bombs?

The average White man has no innate propensity to hate Negroes or throw bombs. Every race has criminal elements and neurotics, including the White race, and these are often inflamed by agitators and destructive legal decisions based on deception.

Please comment on the conflict between your views and the

*views of Christ [1] and the founding fathers of this country,[2] that
is, if there is a conflict?*

[1]All men are brothers; [2] all men are created equal.

1. I can answer this point in the words of Weyl and Possony
in their *Geography of Intellect,* 1963: "If my brother is a cripple,
do I treat him as if he were physically sound? If he is mentally
retarded, does a brotherly attitude consist in pretending that he is
normal?"

2. The phrase you quote is taken from the Declaration of
Independence which was written by Thomas Jefferson at a time
when most Negroes were chattel property. Here is what Jefferson
thought about the Negro race: "Nothing is more certainly written
in the book of fate than that these people are to be free; nor is it
less certain that the two races, equally free, cannot live under
the same government."

*I respect your faith in the many authors quoted. Perhaps
the majority or even all are correct. However, should these differences, if they exist, mean that we treat an individual of this
different race other than as an equal? I may be idealistic and no
doubt prejudiced, but treating the Negro race as unequal can in
no way help them and will only help us Whites in dislike for the
colored person. On the other hand, treating the Negro as an equal
may indeed help his race and ours by giving him a chance to show
his worth. Thank you for an intelligent and relatively unemotional
presentation. It will make many of us weigh our beliefs again,
which cannot hurt any individual.*

Thank you for your comments. But the evidence indicates
that the average Negro cannot compete against the average White
man and that throwing him into competition does not help him.

Moreover, do you really think that forcing the White children
of the South, at the point of a bayonet and against the wishes
of their parents, into schools with a race which the balance of the
evidence today indicates to be 200,000 years behind them in
evolutionary grade, is idealistic? Do you really think turning the
Negro loose in the Congo to rape, murder and torture nuns is

idealistic? Is this what you mean by giving him a chance to show his worth?

Talking about race differences just angers and humiliates the Negro. What good can come from it?

The correct answer to your question requires an examination of the cause of the anger. The trouble is this: The Negro has been told by White liberals that his difficulties are the result of White injustice. This has inflamed him against the White man. It has also led to a certain sympathy for, and encouragement of, Negro aggressiveness on the part of bemused Whites among the general population.

Sensing these things, the Negro has naturally indulged himself in a totally fallacious fantasy. The average Negro honestly believes himself the victim of injustice and oppression, whereas the truth is he has had endless help from the White race. In America the Negro has received more aid than anywhere else in the world. Any Negro who doubts this should ask himself why, if he dislikes it here, he does not return to Africa where he can enjoy the culture his own race created.

The Negro's present behavior is entirely a taught reaction based upon fraud. The cure for this sort of sickness is to teach the truth.

How can we tell the Negro he is inferior, particularly when we add that the inferiority is genetic and therefore hopeless?

As I said at the outset, the use of the word "inferiority" in this area is the result of deliberate calculation on the part of White leftists. It is intended to arouse anger instead of reason in the reader or listener. The Negro race is a younger race than the White race—consequently it has certain limitations. In the broadest philosophical sense this is not inferiority, and it need not be called inferiority in any sense. Kindness, tact and goodwill would avoid the word, but the leftists betray their true colors by using it often—albeit in a sort of inverted context by putting it in the mouths of their opponents.

Secondly, it should be obvious that genetic inequality is almost universal. It is just as real intra-racially as interracially. I am aware of my genetic inferiority to many men in many ways. But I do not consider that this makes my life hopeless. I try to work within my limitations to make the most of what capacities I may possess. You have often heard the old saying "Life's not in holding a good hand but in playing a poor one well." That is the real achievement, the only true title to respect, the only genuine source of human dignity. I do not ask the government to help me force myself into the company of those who are genetically my superiors, or who may differ from me in other ways.

Would not the Negro gain by social association with the White race and ought not the White race freely to grant such association to the Negro?
I suppose I might "gain" if I had lunch twice a week at the White House, spent my vacations with the British Prime Minister and dined every night with the Pope. But this is not the kind of association I have earned or that I would expect to find mutually profitable. Without such mutuality the relationships would soon become strained.

Should not human differences be tolerated by all mankind in order that we may live peaceably together?
There is a distinction between tolerating differences on the one hand and, on the other, so organizing a society that the attributes constituting the differences are incorporated or absorbed as between a lower and a higher culture. Tolerance in such a case simply results in the destruction of the higher and superior culture.

How do you know our culture is superior?
Because the other cultures envy us, not vice versa. They not only want our money and other fruits of our achievement; they would like to enter our society if they could. You will seldom find a Negro who cares to move back to Africa. At least I have never met one.

If your sort of attitude were generally accepted it would cut off most of the current programs to help the Negro. Comment?

Not if my position is understood. I have pointed out repeatedly that I believe the Negro problem varies with the genetic spectrum and that the solutions must be equally various, locality by locality. As far as one can indulge in broad generalities I would say that voluntary non-social integration is desirable—forced social integration, undesirable. I have no objection whatever, indeed I would urge, the humanitarian to gratify his passion for good works by fighting in the mass media, the churches and the schools for an attitude of greater cooperation between the races, an attitude based on reality instead of fraud.

I believe much can be done to assure the exceptional Negro higher-echelon jobs, but the statistics and the scientific facts are clear that the average Negro is not now, and in the foreseeable future cannot be made, equal to the average White man in his capacity to handle higher-echelon jobs. To demand that he be forced into such jobs, or to make him dissatisfied with lesser jobs, is a sure road to riots.

There are today literally millions of jobs going begging in the field of domestic service, which is a natural field for the average Negro but for which he has neither the training nor the desire, having been taught by the White leftist to disdain both the work and the available wage. The relationship as to both employment and welfare which existed for generations between White and Negro families in the South was almost ideal because it was based upon reality. The White family took a cradle-to-grave responsibility for the Negro family and the latter repaid the former in faithful service.

In those areas where the Negro population is a small percentage of the total, I believe voluntary, *not federally compelled,* integration of public accommodations is a valid objective. Where the Negro population is a large percentage I think the problem then begins to vary with the kind of public accommodation. It is far too variable a matter for us to attempt to cover every possible situation with one rule, which is why the decision should be left to local authorities.

You often use the word "leftist". What do you mean by this term?

All generalities have their exceptions and all definitions are dangerous. Keeping this in mind, I would say that a leftist is a person who believes in taking the money out of the pocket of the man who earned it and giving it to somebody else. To be a bit more cynical, often he is a man who seeks legal ways of stealing from the top in order to buy the support of the bottom. He is a man who lays stress on the Commandment "Love thy neighbor" and never mentions the Commandments "Thou shalt not covet" or "Thou shalt not steal."

The driving motivation behind the hard-core leftist, as distinguished from the bemused humanitarian, is envy—he uses the Commandment concerning love as a mask to cover his violation of the Commandments concerning theft and covetousness. Envy takes a multitude of forms and expressions. You will find relatively few men who have built their own fortunes in the hard-core group, although there are some of the former in the bemused group, and many whose fortunes are inherited.

Envy, I believe, operates widely among the academicians and intellectuals, who instinctively resent the rewards of successful industrial enterprise. The qualities of leadership, courage and executive ability—which compel one to face reality in dealing with people as well as things—are relatively rare among them. A man who is responsible for getting things done in an organization of other men in the face of ruthless economic or natural facts, is seldom by nature a leftist, but his achievements are always the source from which the leftist dispenses his liberality.

Envy of our Anglo-American civilization, and of the qualities of mind and character which built it, is widespread among certain races, and operates in the same way—there is a strong drive to dispense its benefits to everybody while denigrating the source as "Puritan" or "reactionary".

Money is not the only thing which can be coveted or stolen. It is just as possible to steal a culture, or rather to debase it, since with integration a race without the capacity to adapt can only destroy—it cannot possess. The leftist in the racial area seeks to take by force the hard-earned and long cherished customs, traditions, standards and other social and political attributes of our White society and distribute and share them with Negroes. His insinct here is the same as his instinct in the economic area.

Let me review for a moment the broader aspects of this instinct. Pity for the deserving poor and hostility toward the sort of buccaneering economic tyranny which characterized the late nineteenth century are healthy motivations. They spring from a desire for justice which is one of our higher human qualities and which all reasonable men are willing to express in the form of some taxation and levies on the public treasury.

What the leftist does is to kidnap this quality and use it to lead people across the boundary beyond justice, even beyond all reasonable mercy, to the point where the taxing power, drafts upon the public treasury and other laws are used to attract the votes of people who have no objection whatever to letting someone else meet their bills or pay the price of their mistakes. Soon a habit is formed, one of the most unbreakable habits known to man, and the beneficiaries come to expect the donations as a right. Thus the taxation of success, enterprise and thrift to support failure, indolence and improvidence is institutionalized.

If the society is a rich one with large accumulations of wealth from the past, or with a highly productive technology developed by its more intelligent members, the leftist is in his glory for many years. His popularity with the masses knows no bounds, and more and more intellectuals join his ranks as they build ingenious excuses for abandoning the old verities. Only by degrees does the irreversibility of the trend become apparent. The heritage of earlier days, enshrined in hundreds of ideals and principles, the experience of a thousand years of trial and error in building and controlling a free society, slowly are eroded away. Only at long last is it discovered that a civilization has been destroyed.

Could you tell us your qualifications for the statement that Christ never recommended integration? Are you a Christian?

My qualifications are a reading of the Bible. I am a Christian. For nearly two thousand years, in fact up until 1954, nobody supposed Christianity required integration. The idea is a recent discovery, trotting obediently along behind the Supreme Court decision. Like much of religious dogma it is an overlay on the original, put there by very fallible men, and none has proved so fallible or so weak—I might say such sheep—as the majority of our religious leaders when it comes to the race problem. I take off my hat to the minority, North and South, who still stand four square for truth. As for the rest, they have done much to discourage the confidence of honest and informed people in their leadership.[30]

When I have raised the point that the Negro problem should be solved in the area of the personal relationships between men because you cannot by law give a man a heart, I have been met by the reply: "But by law you can restrain the heartless." Have you any counter-argument?

The flaw is in your own position which assumes that the segregationist is heartless. As we have seen from the findings in the *Stell* and *Evers* cases, the segregationist is actually kinder to the Negro than the integrationist.

While there certainly are White men who are unjust and discourteous to Negroes, they are not the source of the Negro problem. Such men are unjust and discourteous to members of their own race when the opportunity arises. I do not believe the *average* White man is any more unkind or rude to Negroes than he is to other White men with whom he has little in common.

Negroes are mostly poor. Since our Western civilization is founded upon the principle of compassion and charity toward the poor, the government ought to take an active part in carrying out this ideal.

The difference between the government and the individual functioning in this area is that when the government acts it is no

30. For a discussion of one of the more reprehensible distortions of history by Richard Emrich, Episcopal Bishop of Michigan, on June 4, 1961, see my speech at Jackson, Miss., on Oct. 26, 1961, *Congressional Record*, Jan. 25, 1962, Vol. 108, No. 10, pp. 830-831.

longer charity. Charity is voluntary. The government takes by force from some to give to others. A certain amount of such taking may be generally agreed upon by all reasonable men to accomplish the relief of those wider dislocations which only the government can reach.

But there is an inevitable tendency for a government unrestricted by constitutional limitations to give more and more to please more and more voters. It becomes again a case of robbing the top to buy the support of the bottom. There is a word for this, but it isn't charity.

We as the world's most prosperous nation should be grateful for our blessings and share them gladly with other countries. You are evil and selfish.

Consider a parable. A man goes out into a desert wilderness and, by dint of effort and skill, digs himself a well. In time he develops an oasis with fruit trees and shade.

One day a caravan descends upon him with hundreds of people, all demanding water, fruit and shade. All wish to settle permanently around him but none wishes to dig his own well, nor has the capacity to do so.

Therefore the original settler agrees to supply all the others, and before long neither he nor anyone else has anything. The well has gone dry. The oasis is ravaged. The place is a desert again.

The water, the fruit and the shade in this parable are not to be interpreted literally. They are the water of enterprise, the fruit of intelligence, the shade of self-control—all the elements that go to make up a stable, free society.

My point is that neither the spiritual nor the material resources of our civilization are unlimited. We *cannot* support the world on our own standard of living, and unless we conserve within reason the products of our culture, neither we nor the world will progress.

I am not a communist, but I believe their concept "from each according to his ability, to each according to his need" is a sound, humanitarian objective. If not, why not?

Picture a thug with a blackjack on a dark street. He slugs a passerby and steals his wallet. The thug has a need, the passerby has the ability to satisfy it. So the wallet changes hands. Such a philosophy can only result in hanging a millstone around the necks of diligence, enterprise and foresight while encouraging indolence, shiftlessness and theft.

As a matter of fact this is precisely what is happening throughout the nation today. The more we excuse and appease evil, the more crime increases. The more we subsidize illegitimate children, the more illegitimate children are born. The more permissive we are in our attitudes towards a disorderly society, the more disorderly our society becomes.

In all these areas we see unfold a transparent truth, namely: Crime and demoralization are the fruits of the looseness of thought and attitude inherent in the communist concept you mention.

You have no conception of a world united in brotherhood. You are fifty years behind the times.

I have already said something about brotherhood, but I will add one thing more. Love, like charity, begins at home. A man who loves all countries, and all races, as much as he loves his own, is like the man who loves all women as much as he loves his wife. He merits suspicion. I have seldom seen the matter put better than by William Massey in his article "The New Fanatics," [31] in the section entitled "Whither Brotherhood?" To that question Mr. Massey answers:

"Nowhere. The current furor over brotherhood is compounded of fallacy and foolishness. For it is fallacy to believe that men are no longer separated by enduring differences, and it is foolishness wilfully to believe this fallacy. Yet this fallacy is the basis for the present campaign for brotherhood. This is not a campaign by men who love humanity, but by men obsessed with a vision. Their vision is of a united mankind marching toward a Utopian

---

31. This article was originally published in *The Mankind Quarterly*, 1963, Vol. IV, No. 2. It is available in revised booklet form from the National Putnam Letters Committee, *supra*, p. 19n.

world. It is the stylized, inhuman vision they love, not man. They do not look at man dispassionately, or even with affection, to see his condition and help him. Instead they preach a mystic brotherhood of man that is both goal and means to the goal. This brotherhood is not reached by good will, understanding and tolerance. It is a fanatic's dream, a will-o'-the-wisp that gives them the self-righteousness to vent their hatreds with a clear conscience. Better an honest enemy than so strange a brother."

MISCELLANEOUS

Have not scientists throughout history often been persecuted when their discoveries conflicted with popular views? How about Galileo?

There has never been a situation, not even in the case of Galileo, where the tampering with scientific truth has been as dangerous as it is today, because never before has the tampering been used as a tool of social revolution and genocide.

If Negroes are innately inferior, why must they be so carefully segregated by law and custom? In any competition, they would lose. If the "inferior" Negro can drag down the "superior" Caucasian race, then perhaps the latter wants to be dragged down.

The informed White man is not concerned with Negro "competition." He is concerned with the difference in average evolutionary grade and the ultimate effect of genetic infusion. As for the inferior dragging down the superior, let me quote you William Harvey's lines: "Far more and abler operations are required to the fabric and erection of living creatures than to their dissolution, and plucking of them down. For those things that easily and nimbly perish are slow and difficult in their rise and complement."

I am puzzled by the attitude of churchmen nowadays who seem to think the Christian religion demands they support policies which are certain to lead to the aforesaid plucking down. They appear to care little for the heritage bequeathed them by their forebears, or for the millenniums of self-denial and self-discipline that have been a part of the growth of Western civilization and its codes of honor and decency.

They nimbly forget the effort and sacrifice—and the handing
on of a torch—through countless generations. This is the trust
which they now propose to abandon. But before they dissipate
so many of those values which their ancestors committed to their
keeping, let such as these remember the words of Paul to the
Corinthians: "It is required in stewards that a man be found
faithful."

*If you have evidence in writing of the cases of academic sup-
pression, why do you not expose these universities by naming
names? If you are shielding the individual involved—are they all
lacking the courage of their convictions—this seems curious to
say the least.*
There is nothing curious about it. When a man's livelihood
and social standing are at stake, he naturally shrinks from jeopar-
dizing both. You are naïve if you think otherwise. On the other
hand there are a number of scientists, several of whom I have
cited, who, because of exceptional courage, or retirement status,
or both, have consistently spoken out.

*If White standards are so much higher than Negro standards,
why are there so many mulattoes?*
Although I have said it over and over again, let me remark
once more that when we speak of race we speak of averages.
The average White man is not responsible for the mulatto.

*If Whites developed before Negroes, why do Whites have more
hair than Negroes and most animals have a lot of hair?*
There seems no doubt that the best criteria of evolutionary
grade are in the brain, not in the quantity of hair. The salamander
has no hair.

*All facts you have presented seem to be based on majority
standards. Wouldn't these facts be treated differently if the Negro
was a majority race? Decisions therefore are not absolute, but
relative to a majority's point of view. An example: if 60 per cent
of the people on the earth call a certain fruit an orange and the*

other 40 per cent call the same fruit an apple, who is right?

If the Negro were a majority race we would be living under conditions similar to the Congo or Haiti. Do you recommend this? Or I might put the matter another way: Who envies the other's culture the most, the White man or the Negro?

a. *Would you consider President Johnson a Communist or Socialist because of his stand on civil rights?*

b. *Are Jews and Orientals mentally inferior to Whites?*

c. *Do you consider college students working in Mississippi Communistists or Socialists?*

a. No. In my opinion his stand on civil rights is due partly to ignorance (which in turn results from a lack of the intellectual initiative to investigate the matters we have been discussing) and in part to political expediency.

b. Chinese and Japanese school children test about the same as White children in Hawaii and California. I have already said that Jews (who are not a race) test as well as or better than American non-Jews "on verbal" tests; somewhat below on manipulative tests.

c. I would guess that their motives vary.

Provided the environment of the Negro and White were completely reversed, what would be the end result in crime, etc?

Within a generation the White and Negro would be back where they are now. Let it be repeated: The Negro's nature and behavior are the primary cause of his environment, not vice versa.

The Moynihan Report[32] *shows that most of the Negro's troubles stem from the fact that a much larger percentage of Negro families are headed by women than is the case with White families. This is due to slavery which destroyed the sense of responsibility in Negro fathers, and left them no incentive to care*

---

32. Daniel P. Moynihan, *The Negro Family: The Case for National Action*, 1965, Office of Policy Planning and Research, U.S. Department of Labor.

for their wives or children. This is one more injustice done by Whites to Negroes. Have you any answer?

You are aware of the ten exhibits I have offered on the evolutionary status of the Negro. I now ask you to weigh the slavery explanation you have just given me against the fact that individual control over the instinct of sexual promiscuity is a measure of civilized development. The more sexual promiscuity you have in any society the less apt you are to find fathers at home caring for the children of any particular woman.

It is true that African tribes observe their customs faithfully. But in Africa you have both polygamy and at the same time severely repressive measures to keep the individual within the confines of tribal discipline. The real test comes when these measures are relaxed and the attempt is made to fit the Negro into the framework of Western civilization.

We approach the heart of a major matter here. Whether it be in an individual, or in the average of a race or any other group, personal dedication to one's family—to one's wife and children—is a profound barometer of evolutionary grade. In the family complex the traditions and experience of the past are cherished, while the future is foreseen and secured. The better this is done, the more advanced is the civilization of which the individual is a part. It involves self-control and the putting of long-range values ahead of temporary indulgence, without which few such values are ever achieved and which in itself is a mark of an advancing evolution.

Heaven knows, the average White man is inadequate enough in this area. But if you think he is in the same class with the average Negro you are indeed hypnotized.

a. *The White illegitimacy rate is increasing along with that of the Negro.*

b. *Whites are richer than Negroes and consequently can afford abortions. The figures on abortions prove this. That explains their lower rate. Comment?*

a. There has been a rise from 2% to 3% in the White rate between 1940 and 1963, but to compare this rise to the Negro situation is ridiculous. In the same period the Negro rate rose from 17% to 24%. The rate increased by 11 per thousand among Whites, 68 per thousand among Negroes. The Negro rate is now eight times the White rate. In other words, although the improvement in the Negro's condition in the last twenty-five years has been relatively large, there has been a sharp relative decline in the moral sector of his behavior.

b. Undoubtedly relative abortions, and relative caution and responsibility in other respects, will account for some part of the difference in rate. But this in itself is due to the inherent nature of the races. Also you must remember that in all states of the Union abortions to prevent illegitimacy are illegal and performed in secrecy. Consequently when someone tells you that White women have more abortions to *prevent illegitimacy* than Negroes you should ask him where he gets his figures.

On the other hand, do you honestly suppose that this explanation accounts for an *eight times* difference in rate?

Suppose you were a Negro. How would you feel and what would you do?

It would depend upon the type of Negro I was. If I were an American citizen but genetically close to West Africa I would find work within my limitations and be contented in it. I have pointed out that there are millions of jobs going begging in domestic service today simply because Negroes have either been taught to suppose they are too good for domestic work, or else demand a wage the average White family cannot afford to pay. Consequently many such Negroes loiter or riot in slums, cursing society, and hugging the illusion that they are the victims of injustice. Instead they are the victims of a false conception of themselves, and the only injustice in the situation is due to the leftists who misled them.

If, on the other hand, I were an overlap Negro, or a mulatto, I would choose between a career of leadership in the American Negro community as a business or professional man—or, in the event I had an adventurous streak in me, I would qualify myself for service in Africa among the "emerging" peoples there, helping to carry to my racial homeland the civilizing influences I had absorbed in America.

This does not mean that I would welcome the political and social chaos that presently exists in Africa. I would certainly pray for an awakening among White men which would restore a semblance of order. The present fallacy of supposing that African tribes have any conception of self-government or the meaning of a free society, or can be expected to acquire it in a few decades, is not conducive to constructive work. I would hope for a return to the controlled conditions I mentioned in *Race and Reason* under mandates from an association of free and civilized nations, so that Negro pioneers from the United States might not be plunged into a total jungle.

Should such become the case, I would find it an attractive field for a career. With law and order restored, and with protection for investments of White capital, there would exist both an appeal to altruism and to enlightened self-interest. A Negro could not only be of service to his people but make money too.

How can you talk about the Negro absorbing civilizing influences in America when you see the way he is treated here?

The Negro has more advantages and opportunities in America than anywhere else on earth. If I were a Negro, I would hope to profit by them, as many Negroes have profited, instead of drifting downward into slums or whining about an environment which my race's own limitations created. I have no sympathy with writers like James Baldwin who focus on the dregs of Negro America, thereby disclosing precisely the negative attitude which keeps so many Negroes where they are.

Let us be clear on one point. The White man owes the Negro nothing. If there are any debts outstanding, they are owed by the Negro to the White man. The Negro owes the White man hospitals, medicines, schools, food, opportunity, and a standard of living he could not possibly have acquired for himself. Most of the Negroes in America today would not even exist if their ancestors had not been brought here from Africa. The majority of these ancestors would have been wiped out by savagery.

With such facts in mind it is high time Negroes like Baldwin began looking both at what they owe America and at what they can gain from America with a more positive attitude and a shrewder self-evaluation. America is a great country and a good country—and was, before 1954. Its people are tender and compassionate beyond any other on earth. If the Negro has trouble here, he had best examine himself for the answer.

It is a validated fact that you would not be here if you didn't have a mother. This is the same as the Negro's position—he wouldn't be here if he weren't the descendant of slaves brought to America. What differences does this make on White supremacy? Are you inferior to your mother because she was here first?

I am here because my mother lived in a civilization which made it possible for her to survive. Had the ancestors of our American Negroes been left in Africa, it is certain that many of them would not have survived and consequently their descendants would not be here. I did not say that this had anything to do with what you call "White supremacy." I made the point in connection with the debt the Negro owes the White man.

All your suggestions are based on Whites making the plans and decisions. What makes you think the Negro would accept such a program?

Your question reminds me of a remark in a letter I received the other day from a White man in Central Africa. He said a friend of his, another White man, had just returned from the United States and had reported that "in America the Negro has the White man on the run."

Judging by the attitude inherent in your question I would suspect the report is correct. At least I would say that the Negro has the bemused White liberal on the run. It is a disgusting spectacle. Consider it honestly.

Here is the White race, both in Britain and America, possessed of the greatest technology on earth, enjoying the fruits of a relatively advanced evolutionary status, not only as regards forms of government, standards of living and other traditions, but as to the power to enforce its will. Yet it cowers before something like the Watts riot, rushing about for solutions that will prevent a recurrence in Los Angeles or elsewhere, placating and appeasing with talk about hundreds of millions of White money that must be spent to avoid the horrors otherwise in store. This cowering and bootlicking takes place before the threats of a race 200,000 years behind the White race in evolutionary grade with no technology whatever and no force remotely comparable.[33]

It seems incredible except for the hypnosis. It brings to mind another comment made by a prominent Englishman who went to New Delhi to attend a meeting after India achieved dominion status and apologized to the assembly with the remark that no British subject could humble himself sufficiently to express his regret for the wrongs which had been done to the Indian people.[34] To say this in India, in the face of all that Britain has done for India, is bad enough. To say it in Africa or America to a race which is far more retarded than the Indians is ten times worse. There is no way of accounting for it except by an assumption of guilt based on a totally false conception of the facts.

So in answer to your question, I say it is for the White man to tell the Negro what he will accept, not vice versa. Not only was this nation built by the White man but he is still in the majority. If the Negro wants to live here, let him adapt to our requirements and decisions.

You seem to object to the United Nations as a source of mandates for reconstituted colonialism. You suggest an association

33. An interesting confirmation of this judgment is afforded by a paper delivered on December 28, 1965, before the American Historical Association's 80th Annual meeting in San Francisco by Prof. Elliott M. Rudwick of Southern Illinois University. Prof. Rudwick said in part: "One reason for the explosion of the last two summers has been the awareness that whites are to some degree in retreat, that white mobs in the North no longer organize to attack, and that to a large degree the frustrated Negroes in slums like Watts can get away with acts of destruction." Conditions appeared to be changing in the fall of 1966.

34. Speech by Viscount Stansgate, formerly Major Wedgewood Benn, as head of a British Parliamentary Delegation, reported to me by a member of the audience.

of free and civilized nations—would you define your word "civilized"?

Civilization is a matter of degree. There has never before been any problem among the great powers as to who belonged in their group, and there would be none today were it not for the cleavage between the free and communist worlds.

The free nations of Western civilization are throttling themselves in their attempts to accommodate communism. A separate organization of free countries seems to me the only solution, keeping the United Nations as a debating society for the free and communist countries combined. When I speak of a mandated colonial system I refer to one which would be set up under such an organization of free powers—these are the powers which previously administered most of the colonies which are now falling apart.

I do not hesitate to express my belief that the scientists who, over the last 30 years, have misled the British and American public and their governments on the capacity of backward races for democratic self-government are responsible for the dissolution of colonial control. In this sense they are as guilty of the horrors in the Congo as if they had put the gun to the head of Carlson or the knife to the throat of the nuns.

I will go further and suggest that, had it not been for these scientists and their equalitarian, socialist-motivated propaganda, the ideological and political entering wedge which communism is achieving in Africa and elsewhere would not be a menace today. For this reason many people are coming to feel that there is a perceptible communist influence in our educational establishment. Perhaps it was not entirely a coincidence that the FBI recently arrested a research associate in "social" anthropology at Harvard, a man named Zborowski, on a charge of perjury growing out of the Bureau's investigation of a Soviet spy ring.

You often speak of the scientific hierarchy. Isn't there also a hierarchy of money and success which tends to discriminate against the less successful, both Negro and White?

There used to be. But for the last generation, in this country at least , the shoe has been on the other foot; any man of wealth or position who fails to support racial equalitarianism finds himself ostracized by his own class. He may avoid the issue, but he cannot, for instance, actively oppose integration.

For many years socialists, communists, and left-wingers generally have been preaching the guilt of the older regimes and picturing them as rascals both in matters of business and in their racial attitudes. Now it looks as if our moneyed and successful classes had come to believe it. They appear to be ashamed that they are not failures, too. Indeed all the governments of the Western world seem anxious to apologize for our civilization to all those to whom they have tried to give it and who are proving themselves incapable of absorbing it. In other words, our ruling classes are not only ashamed of segregation, they no longer take pride in anything unrelated to "liberal" programs, government aid and a renunciation of faith in individual self-sufficiency.

Having had some experience as an observer both in business and in the academic life—both with men who have achieved money and success under our free-enterprise system and with those who have risen high as liberal intellectuals in the academic world and government—I would like to assure the former that they have no need to apologize to the latter. Our productivity as a nation and our unequalled standard of living are not primarily the result of government nor the socialist ideology, nor are they the result of organized labor, any more than Hamlet is the product of the pen Shakespeare used to write it. They are the product of the initiative, organizing ability, daring and intelligence of our business entrepreneurs, managers, inventors and engineers.

I have repeatedly heard intellectuals, and occasionally even professional men such as lawyers closely associated with business enterprise, disparage the talents of the executive at the top as if he were essentially only an ornament and all the real work were done elsewhere. Much of it of course is, but I can assure the critics of our capitalistic system that the difference between the Russian standard of living and ours does not lie in a comparison between our lawyers and theirs, or our intellectuals and theirs, or our labor and theirs. It lies in the difference between our industrial leaders and theirs, and the free-enterprise system under which ours operate.

There is a quality in the shrewd business man compounded of self-control, patience, disciplined thinking, balanced judgment, and the courage to take risks. He represents a combination of common sense, leadership, and a capacity for action which is the primary source of our achievements as a nation and our standard of living. Independence, self-confidence and decisiveness are his hallmarks. He is worth every penny he is paid.

And he is the antithesis of everything that socialism, communism and the typical left-winger stand for.[35] It is time he reasserted himself in our society, instead of apologizing for his existence and his accomplishments. If he "discriminates against the less successful, both Negro and White," it is because he cannot treat everybody alike and get anything done.

Please understand that in paying this tribute to the spark-plug in the cylinder I do not intend to disparage the rest of the engine. Nor am I unaware of the beneficial role which government has come to play at both the state and federal level in policing the business buccaneer in his relation to the stock market, to labor, to his competitors and to the public. I realize the soundness of regulatory theory and I have experienced its advantages in practice. There is, however, no connection between this kind of regulation and the equalitarian ideology.

Do you believe that the world is confronted with a class war with race overtones, or a race war with class overtones?

This is one of the more difficult questions that students of modern history have to debate. If we must use the word war,

---

35. For a confirming sidelight, see John W. Gardner, "The Antileadership Vaccine," being a part of the Annual Report of the Carnegie Corp. of N.Y. for 1965. Gardner was Secretary of Health, Education, and Welfare at the time this report appeared, although formerly president of the corporation. In the essay he notes the inclination of intellectuals to picture the leader as having "tasted the corrupting experience of power" and their policy of "immunizing" students "against any tendency toward leadership."

then I would say that the ratio varies with the area considered. On a world scale it is probably a race war with class overtones, simply because race and class so closely coincide in many areas— and wherever this is true I think race is the more powerful force. In England it is a class war with race overtones.

In the United States I would call it about fifty-fifty. If I had to fall on one side or the other I might choose the race war with class overtones. However, no matter what you decide, establishing the scientific truth concerning human differences and educating all the people in regard to them is essential to any solution.

There need be no war where enlightened justice controls the policies of a society, both intra- and interracially. But you will have ceaseless war where you inflame one side with groundless expectations and imaginary wrongs while you plunder the other side in the process. You will likewise have ceaseless war where the top plunders the bottom.

You have criticized the South for not taking action to clear up the race-differences point. I am a Southerner, and there are three things I was taught as a child that a gentleman never did, namely, insult a woman, be cruel to an animal or hurt the feelings of a Negro.

This is all very well until the woman blackmails you, the animal goes for your throat, or the Negro leadership begins to undermine your civilization. I must remark that in my opinion you have waited far too long to defend everything that as a gentleman you were taught to value.

As a Southerner I feel it is up to Northerners to discuss race differences. We are too deeply involved with the Negro and will be called bigots and racists if we mention these differences.

Unfortunately this is true, but on the other hand there is scarcely a Northern political leader who has had any experience until recently with the Negro problem or has cared enough about it to inform himself. Traditionally the Negro is a Southern, not a Northern, problem. People tend to look to Southern leaders for an explanation of the Negro's status in our society.

To illustrate the way Northerners react to your states' rights and constitutional arguments (simply because they are misinformed about your real argument), let me quote you parts of a letter concerning the Civil Rights Bill written by Bishop Coadjutor Harry Lee Doll of Baltimore to his diocese: "It is clearly evident that the issue in this legislation is not that of States' Rights against the encroachment of dictatorial Federal powers, as men like Governor Wallace would have us believe. The real aim of the opponents of this legislation is the continuation of an outworn and immoral system of racial separation and degradation. Against this I protest in the name of the God and Father of us all, whose love and concern for all mankind regardless of race or color or creed has been manifest in Jesus Christ our Lord."

Here is a man who at least appears [36] to be bemused as to the facts, a man of great influence with the public, and a man typical of thousands of other religious leaders. *This man's arguments you never meet,* and no one else has as much at stake in doing so as you do.

I am a Southern political leader. Do you honestly expect me to go out and say the Negro is inferior?

Great Scott! How many times must I point out that you do not need to use either that word or that concept! The Negro is a younger race. The public has been deceived as to this fact. The evidence in *Stell* and *Evers* and their companion cases all points to damage to the Negro as well as to the White child from integration, because of differences not only in I.Q. but in subject interest and problem approach. This evidence has been concealed, and false evidence has been made the basis of a Supreme Court decision which is undermining the health of our society. These are the things you talk about, not "inferiority".

Let politicians in the North do it. They do not have Negro families in their homes who have been there for generations.

---

36. For polls as to the actual extent of public deception on race differences see *supra,* p. 5n.

Northern politicians have constituents who are more bemused
than yours. If these politicians started talking they would be
retired at the next election.

*Southern politicians have done their best already. I remember
Governor Barnett wrote a letter to every governor of every state
in the country recommending they read, and urge the public to
read, Race and Reason. What more do you want?*

I am deeply grateful to Governor Barnett and I have had the
utmost cooperation from other Southern governors, both in the
promotion of *Race and Reason* and in affording me platforms and
endorsement for speeches I have made in the South.

But this is not what I mean. What I say on this matter is of
minor importance. What they could say would be listened to,
particularly if they acted in concert, as for example by joint mani-
festoes or on *national* television programs—or if they spoke individually when they had national attention at the time of some
crisis such as Oxford or Selma. These are the opportunities which
always seem to be missed.

*Get yourself elected to the Senate and maybe you will learn
something about politics. If we Southerners raise the question
of race differences we will lose the sympathy and help of Northern
conservatives who are with us on states' rights, decentralized
government, and similar issues.*

You have me there. And you give me one more ground for
complaint against Northern conservatives. The latter make good
whipping-boys for liberals and that is about all. When they win
elections they do it by providing a slight variant in liberalism;
when they lose, they do it on grounds that make them a public
laughing stock. They appear as hard-bitten, discredited economic
reactionaries, longing for a depression, while the American people
are enjoying the greatest and most widely distributed prosperity
in history.

Meanwhile they leave in the barn the best horse they've got.
The man in the street is burning over the race issue, which is a

winning issue, even among the ignorant.[37] Heavens knows he would burn still more if he knew the truth! In any case it is not so much centralization of power that the man in the street ought to care about as it is centralization of power *in the wrong hands*.

Society today needs more co-ordination than it did fifty years ago. You Southerners know this, and what is more, you like your share of federal assistance. Both you and the Northern public agree there. Your real enemy is not centralized government but *captive* government—government captured by minority groups heading a Negro parade and followed by a bemused mob of dreamy-eyed fanatics, self-serving, short-sighted politicians, and White renegades who prate about racism and practice black racism themselves. These are dividing and confusing our native majority and winning elections on a balance-of-power basis, simply because you and your conservative friends will not give the majority courageous and truthful leadership.

I may not be a politician but my advice to you is: either convert your Northern conservatives or go it alone. Get your country back in the hands of the people who built it, and you will find a consensus on a new compound of liberal and conservative policies.

Let Northerners learn from experience. With the influx of Negroes to Northern cities they are learning already. Why should we expose ourselves to attacks as racists when experience will take care of the situation?

Judging by events in the fall of 1966, you may be right. But I fear you mistake the problem, including the depth of the hypnosis. What we learn from experience depends on how we interpret it. If one has been taught to interpret the behavior of the Negro as simply a reflection of one's own injustice, one gains nothing but deeper hypnosis. Surely you realize that Northern riots have been used as an excuse for more appeasement and more White guilt.

Besides, every year you wait additional students graduate from

37. See *supra*, p. 9.

our colleges, North and South, steeped in the equalitarian deception. This is where the trouble starts and where it must be
stopped soon or you will have no one left to hear you. What is
more, your truth-oriented scientists are growing old.

We have reached the point where the federal government must
act and must purge itself at the same time. All governments
throughout history have been plagued in varying degrees by
financial dishonesty. Contracts have been obtained by personal
influence and bribery, elections have been stolen and fortunes
made at the taxpayer's expense. But I know of no instance in
which *intellectual* dishonesty has been so widespread and is resulting in such damage as is the case today in the area of race.
It is corrupting the integrity of otherwise blameless men to an
extent I have never heard of before.

*What about guilt in the South? Does not the South have good
reason for guilt?*

The South undoubtedly suffers feelings of guilt, both consciously
and unconsciously, concerning the old slavery days and the fact
that currently it does not always deal with the Negro in an ideal
manner. No society ever has. Some forms of non-social segregation might have been discarded earlier. Some types of Southern
White men, as in the North, have treated Negroes with cruel con-
tempt. But there comes to mind a remark once made to me by
a leading Georgia business man who had sat on juries there from
time to time throughout most of his life. He said: "In all my
experience in the courts I have never seen a Negro get justice.
What he got was mercy."

*You have spoken critically of President Johnson's domestic
policies. How do you feel about his foreign policies?*
I believe they have been inept where and to the extent they have
been based on the false premise we have been discussing. There
are two points involved.

First, it is folly to assume *without conclusive proof* that any race
or substock either desires, or is capable of sustaining, a stable,
free society, or, indeed, any stable government.

Second, weak or backward peoples must be protected from communist domination.

The only way I see of meeting both these requirements is through the mandating of control over such peoples by an association of advanced, free nations. If the backward or weak peoples prove themselves capable of genuine democracy, it will eventually become apparent and the mandate can then be vacated. If not, and they seem capable of maintaining law and order under variable degrees of monarchy, the mandate can also be terminated.

The destructive thing is to assume that every race and substock either is or soon will be capable of maintaining a democracy. The result is the collapse of law and order in many areas, followed by loss of life, liberty and property and a consequent end to civilization.

I will repeat what I said in *Race and Reason:* An advanced nation receiving a mandate over a backward area cannot be expected to act without reasonable compensation. Its citizens must be allowed to invest and to see their investments protected. The purpose of the mandate must not be to administer charity, but to distinguish between a fair return and exploitation; the association of nations granting the mandate must police the difference.

I noticed that in his State of the Union address on January 12, 1966, President Johnson said: "A peaceful world order will be possible only when each country walks the way it has chosen for itself. We follow this principle by encouraging the end of colonial rule . . . by continued hostility to the rule of the many by the few —or the oppression of one race by another."

Let us apply these ideas to Central Africa. When the Negro walks the way he has chosen for himself we have ritual murder and the murder of twins; we have the slow cutting of sections from the groin, genitals, arms and faces of live human beings to prepare fetishes, the blood being caught in billy-cans to moisten the fetishes and the operation continuing until the victim dies.

We have human sacrifices for religious purposes; we have boys and girls brought up for years in confined cages, their feet and hands mutilated, so that they can eventually be fitted with claws and become "lion-men", whereupon they are taught to murder in such a way that the victim is believed to have been killed by a lion; we have girl children tortured and terrified by initiation rites so painful that they sometimes die of fright at the prospect of the suffering; we have victims paraded alive before prospective purchasers so that portions of their bodies may be marked off and sold before the victim is slaughtered and eaten; and we have the devouring of nuns to spice the cannibalistic lust for human flesh.[38]

Finally we have governments so unstable that the following report in the *New York Times,* two days before Johnson's speech, has become a commonplace. It records the circumstances surrounding the arrival in Lagos of Prime Minister Wilson for a conference of the British Commonwealth regarding Rhodesia:

"Lagos, Nigeria, . . . This sprawling seaport capital resembled an armed camp as riot police attempted to crush mounting violence by opposition party mobs that seek to embarrass Sir Abubakar.

"Four more were killed last night in the suburb of Mushin, bringing the total weekend death toll to 11 with more than 80 seriously injured. Early this morning one of the two main roads from the airport was blocked by a curtain of flaming gasoline. Policemen later dispersed the demonstrators with tear gas.

"The weekend's political warfare continues an upsurge of violence that has taken more than 100 lives since October's parliamentary elections . . ."

I do not hesitate to say that when a President of the United States can stand before a national audience and take pleasure in asserting that he is "encouraging" these private and public activities, that he is going to show "continued hostility" to the control of them, and that he considers such control "oppression", then that man is in a trance dangerous to a "peaceful world order". He is ignorant of the most elementary realities necessary to wise policy.

Let me see if I can make one other thing clear: when a nation's psyche is eroded by the assumption that although it has struggled through centuries to achieve a standard of civilization,

---

38. See also *Race and Reason,* pp. 43-44, 77.

a stability of government and a degree of power unsurpassed on the face of the earth, it is nevertheless no better than races millenia below it on the evolutionary scale—then that nation loses its self-respect and the respect of all with whom it deals. Its power of leadership and its force of example evaporate. As I have said elsewhere, there is something in the most primitive people that respects and tries to emulate the people or races that know their own worth. They instinctively despise the kowtowing of superiority to inferiority—and so do gangsters and other delinquents, nationally and internationally.

Sad to say the United States in recent years has been in the hands of leaders who lack any understanding of this fact. Had they had it, we would not have gotten into our present predicament throughout the world. We would have called, and successfully called, the hand of communism again and again. There would have been no need to use "the bomb".

My textbook on Africa says "it is the divine right of every people to run its affairs in its own way; self-government, no matter how bad, is more ennobling than non-self-government, no matter how efficient; self-government with danger is infinitely better than subservience with tranquility, and there can be no peace in the world so long as men arrogate to themselves the right to govern without the consent of the governed." Comment?

This is another example of perverted platitudes and bombast. Turning the Negro loose does not result in "self-government"; it always ends in some sort of black dictatorship, through military or one-party rule, which in turn produces exploitation of the average Negro, and other retrogression, far worse than colonial rule. Your quotation sounds as if it were written by a black gangster aching to get his hands on some loot, meanwhile laughing up his sleeve that his abracadabra should work so well.

What troubles me is that any civilized White man should write such nonsense. It discloses a total failure to understand or appreciate his own civilization. He has forgotten, if he ever knew, what centuries of effort it took to develope the capacity for self government. He has no real comprehension of the worth of what his forefathers bequeathed him. Consequently, he can have little pride in himself as the legatee. It does not take many of that sort to start the erosion I spoke of in answering the preceding question.

I am troubled even more by the way this ingratitude is working in our own society. Although I have mentioned it twice before, I will repeat that one of the most alarming things about the current one-man-one-vote slogan is its bearing on the Negro problem. We have, or had, a reasonably healthy, free society which we owed to a healthy inheritance. Now we propose to inject into the blood stream of the body politic, without any control whatever, a virus of Negro votes which, based on the averages, is absolutely certain to undermine our "constitution". It has never failed to produce sickness wherever and whenever it has been tried, throughout the world and throughout history. This should please *White* gangsters in search of loot.

But to get back to the specifics of your question, let me offer an analogy, imperfect but perhaps instructive. Certain parents decide to allow their children to run wild in the neighborhood, without discipline or control, because this is their children's divine right. They argue that delinquency with danger is infinitely more ennobling than subservience with tranquility. Finally these children begin to murder each other by setting fire to one another's clothes. Some parents down the road object to the example being set *their* children but the first parents call them reactionary and threaten to use force to bring the latter's progeny into the carnage. Does his picture gratify you?

If you dislike the present trend of things, what cure do you suggest?

Tell the truth and let the public decide. I have more confidence in the judgment of an informed Anglo-American electorate than does the leftist who shouts "democracy" and "freedom" and then achieves his ends by the roster of deceit I have presented. I will wager that if, for a period of one year, the TV and radio networks, the magazines, book publishers and newspapers, the movies and the theater, in the United States and Britain, were to tell the truth about race differences—were simply to present the evidence on evolutionary grade — you would witness such a political house cleaning as history seldom records.

Speaking of "turning the rascals out", you would observe a turning out of fools and rogues by the thousands. What remained of courts, Presidents and legislators would run bleating like sheep to the opposite side of the issues. You would see an end to the race problem in the United States and abroad within another five years, and a sound administration of the affairs of backward peoples within ten.

But if you now ask me how one goes about telling the truth to millions who have been systematically and purposefully deceived over two generations, when all your channels of instruction are controlled by those responsible for the deceit, I must answer that my visibility into that problem is limited. I can only say, do the best you can.

Are not the Zionists and the international bankers really at the bottom of this brotherhood movement?

It makes little difference now who is at the bottom of it. The problem lies in the world-wide hypnosis on the subject of human equality. This is not confined to any one group, and it can no longer be solved by attacking any one group. We have seen that countless millions sincerely believe in the equalitarian dogma; it influences all their actions, including their votes. It is, if you like, the weapon in the hands of the hard-core leftist. Talking about international bankers today is like talking about states' rights or the Constitution, it is a form of evasion—it avoids the difficult and painful task of awakening the public from their trance.

Your philosophy is Hitlerian. In a world threatened by the atom bomb what possible chance for peace is there unless all races live in mutual respect and equality?

As to Hitler, the perversion of truth by evil men is no reason for abandoning truth, any more than the evils of the Spanish Inquisition were a reason to abandon Christianity. Race, being of the very texture of man's being, is one of the fundamentals of life. Another fundamental is the fact of differences between races in evolutionary grade. Blindly ignoring such matters is a ticket to destruction, especially in an atomic world.

The atom bomb was built by the intelligence and technology of the world's most advanced race. There is some question whether that race is mature enough to control what it created. But one thing is obvious. If the bomb is allowed to drift into the hands of races thousands of years less mature, it will be like putting a loaded gun in the hands of a three year old child.

Meanwhile the world sits with a mixture of bandits and bemused fanatics at the head of the Mongolian and Caucasian peoples, while the Negroes join to make up a rag-tag conglomerate of "independent" countries in the so-called United Nations. It is about as foolish and dangerous a situation as could well be imagined.

The chief responsibility lies with the United States. As the world's most powerful nation, as the builder of the first atom bomb, it was, and is, its duty to lead and to control. It has done, and is doing, neither, except to the extent that it has sponsored and encouraged the dissolution of the colonial system and the substitution for it of the current chaos. The world is seething with racial tensions and other disorders fostered by the official ideology of the United States and Britain. The people who ask your kind of question are responsible for the ideology.

You are a White supremacist. You . . .

At this point I put the question back in the folder and the folder back in the brief case. The pattern was all too obvious and had begun to be nauseating.

With few of these questioners could there by any real discussion. They wished to fight, not to reason. Either that, or they had become emotionally so incapable of facing the truth that any device of diversion, evasion or even deceit was better than genuine analysis.

The common denominator, in their case at least, was intellectual dishonesty. Reasoning on the core question, the question of innate race differences, was a waste of time, and consequently all the rest of the debate became futile. These people simply would not, indeed could not, engage in a sincere search for reality, perhaps because they knew what they would find if they did.

Where, then, was the key, the answer, to the whole fantastic situation?

I rose once more from my desk and paced the room. The first glimmer of dawn came through the windows, but my brief case seemed to offer no solutions. Was it possible there *were* none? On one side stood the reactionaries, the modern Hitlers, the people who gave the leftists the superficial plausibility of their case. On the other stood the bemused humanitarians, oblivious of the destruction they were causing, moving endlessly in circles which returned them to the point where they started, still in a trance.

But gradually it seemed to me I was catching a glimmer of daylight, figuratively as well as literally. I walked over to an eastern window and gazed for a moment toward the sea.

CHAPTER VII

VISTA AT DAYBREAK

Far to the south across the Eastern Way and Bunker Ledge, beyond Marsh Head and Little Cranberry, the flames of sunrise were licking at the shores of Baker Island. Sutton and Great Cranberry were still shrouded in mist. Duck Island was not yet visible. I strained to distinguish the Lewis Rock spar before I remembered I was searching for something harder to find than buoys.

In one respect I was more fortunate than many. In my own lifetime I bridged an unusual number of the years of change. Winston Churchill's "old world in its sunset" was the world of my childhood, years of naïveté in judgment, yet impressionable years which had left some enduring recollections. As far as my reading went, Richard Harding Davis, Rudyard Kipling, Robert W. Service and Zane Grey were all part of my life when I was twelve. In those uncrowded days I could appreciate what Service had in mind when he wrote "the freedom, the freshness, the farness . . . ." One need not have gone to Alaska in those years to find it. I had found it in the Florida of 1910.

I had also witnessed, albeit as a small boy watching, such scenes as Davis depicted in his novels and Gibson in his drawings. Whether in Manila after the Insurrection or in the drawing rooms of New York, I had seen in the flesh the Richard Harding Davis hero and the Gibson girl. At home and in travel both in Europe and the Orient I had savored the mood and spirit of those times.

Then came the first World War, the parades, the cheers, the farewells and afterwards the telegrams that told of the death of a soldier, but meant the death of something else besides, followed by the speak-easy era, the era of the "lost generation", of Scott Fitzgerald's characters in contrast to Davis's, of Warren G. Harding and Teapot Dome in lieu of Theodore Roosevelt, of cartoons like Dove's in the New Yorker, "Let's have the Schubert Serenade

176

and get some dirt into it," of disillusionment with the peace treaties and with the League of Nations.

During the second World War there were fewer parades and fewer cheers, but the same telegrams. Never had there been so many of those messages in so short a span, all delivered between 1914 and 1946, scarcely more than one generation. While the death toll was relatively small in the United States, in England and on the Continent, at the heartland of our Western civilization, it was appalling. Some nine million of the best men of the world's best racial stocks were killed in the first World War alone.

These were the young men who, had they lived, would today be in the seats of power and leadership—not just at the top, but throughout all echelons of influence. War in those days attracted young men whose strength of body and mind was above average, young men with a capacity to set standards. These were the ones who were missed when the time came when they would have been middle-aged and old. From the standpoint of England—our own special heartland—I could well understand Housman's lines:

> "Oh, no, lad, never touch your cap;
> It is not my half-crown;
> You have it from a better chap
> That long ago lay down.

> Turn east and over Thames to Kent
> And come to the sea's brim,
> And find his everlasting tent
> And touch your cap to him."

Yet while such losses must have contributed substantially to the change in values in Europe, they could not be considered the major cause. The United States showed an equal change, and here the losses were not large enough to account for it. The source must lie deeper.

And in searching for it, was not the first step to define just what the differences in those values were? As I turned to my desk, I asked myself the specific question. Having lived through the whole gamut of change and borne witness from my youth to

the tone of the era before the first World War, what was the word
that best conveyed the nature of that tone?

Undoubtedly it was a compound of many factors. But as I
sought in memory to reconstruct the totality of it, my conviction
grew that the chief element was a regard for properly constituted
authority, for law as a symbol of right and of order, and for
earned distinction. It involved the willingness and courage to
look up to the superior and to disdain the inferior—in other
words, to discriminate. It included the capacity both to obey and
to command; a youth learned almost by breathing the air around
him that, to be able to command, he must first learn to obey—
above all to be master of himself.

Such a tone was not conducive to the appeasement of evil. It
involved a capacity for scorn and the nerve to express it. Among
those entitled to do so there was no hesitation in taking command,
no fear of asserting genuine leadership, no reluctance to give
orders or to rebuke insubordination—when the occasion required.
This was not something that prevailed only in the armed forces.
It prevailed between parent and child, between teacher and pupil,
between employer and employee.

Implicit in this tone was the firm and full acknowledgment of
human differences, both individual and racial, both genetic and
self-made. There was no fawning upon nor bootlicking of inferiority or mediocrity. The necessity of earning the desirable things
of life, material and spiritual, and the rights accruing to those
who had earned them, were not controverted. The existence of the
criminal rich did not alter the ideal, nor was it altered by the right
of inheritance. The genes of a man's parents and of his grand-
parents were as much a part of him, as much his property, as his
economic legacy, and on the average contributed to his ability
to use the latter wisely.

Yet still I searched the language for one word to cover the
qualities which the tone produced or which produced the tone. I
could come no closer to it than the noun *honor* which itself was
subject to many definitions and, as I though about it, it seemed to
me that honor was as much the product of the tone as vice versa,
although when once produced the interaction was complete.

Before me among the final notes on my desk lay a hand-written quotation I had found among my father's papers after his death in World War I. It was copied from a novel of those days and it ran as follows:

"Perhaps the most remarkable thing, then, in the character of his mother—which, please God, he will have, or, getting all things else, he can never be a gentleman—was honor. It shone from her countenance, it ran like melody in her voice, it made her eyes the most beautiful in expression that I have ever seen, it enveloped her person and demeanor with a spiritual grace.

"Honor in what we call the little things of life, honor not as women commonly understand it, but as the best of men understand it—that his mother had. . . .

"If he be anything of a philosopher, he may reason that this trait must have made his mother too serious and too hard. Let him think again. It was the very core of soundness in her that kept her gay and sweet. . . . She was of a soft-heartedness that ruled her absolutely—but only to the unyielding edge of honor.

"Beyond this single trait of hers—which if it please God that he inherit it, may he keep though he lose everything else—I set nothing further down for his remembrance since naught could come of my writing.

"But by words I could no more give an idea of what his mother was than I could point him to a few measures of wheat and bid him behold a living harvest."

I did not for one moment propose to suggest that the qualities involved here were prevalent everywhere throughout our Western civilization before the first World War. But I did bear witness to the fact that they were more prevalent then than they are now.

And I would venture the guess that a connection existed between them and what I called the championship held by the English-speaking stocks in the maintenance of stable, free societies. My suspicion grew that when it came to a choice between principle on the one hand and self-interest on the other the *average* man among these stocks would choose principle more often than the *average* man among those stocks who had been less successful in the management of freedom throughout the world—and that he showed it in his face as well as in his actions.

As so often before, one needed to lay stress here on the concept of average, or what the scientists called frequency. It would be ridiculous to imply, for example, that the English-speaking stocks, or even a majority of individuals among them, would *always* choose principle above self-interest. It would be equally absurd to suggest that many among even the least advanced of the world's populations would *never* put principle above self-interest. It was simply that, rare as the occasion might be, the frequency with which an observer would find principle being put above self-interest would be greater in the one case than in the other.

Did this have some relation to evolutionary grade? Like intelligence, there was overlap, but intelligence and integrity were far from synonymous. Could one advance the hypothesis that where intelligence and integrity were combined, there one had the highest evolutionary grade? It was an involved and complex business, but could one not at least say that a stable, free society was the product of both, and that in the proportion that either declined, dry rot was diffused throughout the body politic?

Unless men in a community or a nation had confidence in the integrity of their political, literary and religious leaders, of their news media and their judiciary, they were walking in quicksand. Modern society depended on the assurances people gave to one another, in business, in marriage, in contracts of every sort. Confidence in the honor of one's associates led first to courtesy and respect, and then to sympathy. It oiled the machinery of life from beginning to end. It gave meaning to trial by jury, it validated taxation and above all it led to willing acquiescence by the losers in elections. An honest victory of honest and intelligent men held no terrors for an honest and intelligent minority. But once confidence in a reasonable frequency of integrity was destroyed, the whole basis for stability was gone. The playing fields of Eton had been a symbol. In the narrow sense the symbol was fair play—in the larger sense, honor.

And in the largest sense of all, was this not of the very essence of the success of the English-speaking peoples, in the British Isles, the United States, Canada, Australia, and New Zealand? Evolutionary grade? One asked the question with caution. A precious heritage certainly, something not to be ashamed of in the face of attacks from those who had failed where we had succeeded—and had come to us to enjoy the fruits of our success.

I picked up the faded page in my father's handwriting and glanced at it once again.

"A soft-heartedness that ruled her absolutely—but . . ."

But only to the unyielding edge of honor—could one find a better formula for kindness, for love in the context of family, community, nation and world? Was it necessary to spell out every facet? Obviously one did not tell the truth to a child who was dying of an incurable disease, but where the truth was vital to the solution of a problem one faced the truth, if one loved wisely.

So through the whole range of human welfare at home, abroad and in race relations. If one lied here, if one corrupted the minds of a nation, it would be the corruption that would win in the end, not love. It would be the corruption that would spread everywhere and destroy the loving and the loved together.

Compassion as the handmaiden of integrity was the crown of a civilization. Compassion put before integrity meant disaster. Yet the sincere liberal, as well as the hard-core leftist, had reversed the order. Under the mask of the ideal of a more genuine humanity, a wider sharing of the products of our industrial technology and the cultural values of our civilization, he had proceeded to undermine the very values themselves. Hypocrisy, deception, equivocation, and cowardice had taken the place of honor.

Surely what the world now needed more than anything else was a reorientation of the humanitarian impulse after its long perversion by these forces. Smoothing the fur of evil was not kindness. Releasing the forces of savagery in Africa was not goodness. Abdicating one's racial responsibility for leadership was not wisdom. Firmness in the right as God gave us to see the right meant force and power and the exercise of authority and discipline against evil. Once his fact was realized, respect and obedience would follow where it was due, order would return to a befuddled world, and genuine justice and mercy might at last prevail.

Provided—and this was the crux of the matter—provided the truth were told, and there was somebody left to listen.

Chapter VIII

MORNING

Where had the courage gone that was needed to tell the truth? What had destroyed it? Where was the tone that had bred the courage in years gone by? What had destroyed *that?*

Looking frankly at Britain and the United States one beheld a strange situation. One saw an Anglo-American majority battered and divided on other issues, guilt-ridden and bemused by the equalitarian dogma; one observed a mass media saturating the public with a scientific fraud promoted by a hierarchy whose aim was not the search for truth but political propaganda; one found ignorant political and judicial leaders, with mediocre minds and little moral stamina, drawn from a society whose human resources had been emasculated by two generations of compromise and appeasement. These were some of the results of the destruction. But they were not the source.

Nor could the source lie in the humanitarian impulse itself. The drive for social justice and the awakening of sympathy for the unfortunate were both good. Where the train ran off the track was at the equalitarian switch—flashing false signals and manipulated by envy. If there existed one crime more contemptible than any other it was the *use* of good to promote evil. On this siding other trains had been looted and destroyed. Would this one?

But still the question was not on point. Not proximate causes, but the root cause alone could provide the key I sought. In the closing pages of *Race and Reason* I had spoken of the leftward overdrift of the West as justifying to my mind a term Ortega y Gasset had used—"the sovereignty of the unqualified." I had also quoted two sentences from Lord Tweedsmuir: "The gutters have exuded a poison that bids fair to infect the world. The beggar on horseback rides more roughshod over the helpless than the cavalier."

This was strong language, perhaps too strong, but certainly

with the trend toward sympathy with failure—toward encouragement of the underdog—had grown a tendency to disparage the
superior and to fawn upon the inferior. It was not a pretty sight,
this picture of the top abasing itself before the bottom. It did not
improve the bottom, and it meant rapid deterioration at the top.[1]
The good lost respect for goodness, and the bad lost respect for
it, too. Capacity for leadership dwindled, tolerance of evil increased. Was there not here cause enough for the emasculation
of the values which had made the flowering of Western civilization
possible?

In other words, did not the equalitarian dogma, like a rank
growth, contain within itself not only the seeds of its own
proliferation, but of general collapse as well? Was this not the
point where the erosion of both the individual and the national
psyche began?

Let a man be told incessantly that everything he and his forefathers had achieved was largely a matter of chance; that the
poverty and backward condition of other individuals and races
was also largely a question of luck—in fact perhaps even the
fault of himself and his forefathers; that his standards of morals,
fiscal responsibility and personal integrity were no better than
anyone else's; that his civilization was mostly happenstance and
really nothing much to be proud of; that since all humanity were
innately equal, all actual differences must be due to the other
man's misfortune and his own four-leaf clovers—let a man hear
these things often enough and his values were bound to change.

And the change must soon diffuse itself through the family, the
community and the nation. The child must begin to sense it in
the parent, the criminal in the court, the employee in the employer,
the citizen in his leaders. How seldom one saw the word *distinguished* today! How seldom one dared to speak of a man as
discriminating! In other words in condemning the concept of in-

---

1. I cannot forbear quoting once again William Harvey's lines: "Far
more and abler operations are required to the fabric and erection of living
creatures than to their dissolution, and plucking of them down. For those
things that easily and nimbly perish, are slow and difficult in their rise
and complement."

feriority, our society necessarily had had to destroy the concept
of superiority, for one could not exist without the other.

With its destruction had come the death of respect for authority,
of pride in the achievements of the past, of reverence for tradition,
of the wisdom to honor the heritage of one's family, one's race and
one's country. Also had come the death of that quality in superior
men which sprang from confidence not only in their own personal
excellence but in that of their kind and race. This was the most
serious loss of all, for it was an electric quality that had once
communicated itself, with instant conviction, to others. With it
had passed the genius of true leadership, the power to lead up
the hill instead of down, to get a nation "moving again" morally
as well as economically.

It was, in fact, the quality that had given men the courage to
tell the truth. And thus one was back in the circle, which was
just what the hard-core leftist, and the communist, counted on,
and which the bemused humanitarian, and the castrated conservative, obligingly tread like a squirrel in a cage—a vicious circle,
indeed, with just one point where it might be broken: by an
attack on the lie.

So this was the challenge—two generations of false indoctrination to be overcome, an Anglo-American society saturated in a
debilitating fallacy to be cleansed. No doubt in due course the
Supreme Court would forbid the singing of Auld Lang Syne on
New Year's Eve, which would be consistent enough, and would
spare us even the memory of those who had given us all we had.
If ever there was a goose whose golden eggs were being stolen
and which was now in the process of being killed, we were it.

Not many years remained to correct the fallacy. The successors
to the last two generations were in the nursery this very minute,
and in the schools. Luckily life renewed itself in the family and
in the race. There might yet be enough of the genes for honor
left in the human fabric to respond to the truth in a new generation, provided it, too, were not emasculated.

A hard task but a clear one. The sword of truth in the vital
area of race could cut the ground from under both socialism and
communism at one stroke if it were used. Let it be placed in the

hands of honorable men wherever possible, not to injure the defenseless but to restore the strong.

In my own small sphere my testament would have to stand on *Race and Reason* and on this brief review of what had happened since. I had done enough meditating. The time had come to speak.

And the key?

"Beyond this single trait of hers . . . I set nothing further down for his remembrance . . ." I thought of the children of two bemused generations. I could set nothing further down for them.

I heard a knock, the door to my study opened and my wife stood on the threshold smiling wryly. I wondered about that smile, and I wondered still more when she spoke.

"What a waste!" she said.

Could she be referring to a waste of time? Had she perceived my purpose and deemed it hopeless? Then I noticed she was looking over my shoulder, so I turned to follow her glance and understood.

I had been sitting with the lights still on, at my desk and around the room . . .

Yet here it was, broad daylight!

INDEX

ABC-TV, 32
Abortions, 156
Absorption of Negro, 117-18, 121
Africa. *See specific items.*
Alligator, 52, 125
Alpha Tests (World War I), 42
American Anthropological Association, 3, 5, 30-31, 33, 41
American Association for the Advancement of Science (AAAS), 35
American Association of Physical Anthropologists, 32-33
American Dilemma, 70
American Federation of Teachers, 124
American Psychologist, 58n, 60
Anglo-American racial amalgam defined, 11n
Animal Species and Evolution, 54n, 105
Anthropology A to Z, 104n
"Antileadership Vaccine," 163n
Ape, 51, 55
Armstrong, Clairette, 75, 80-81
Army General Classification Test, 115
Atlantic Monthly, 30, 116
Atomic bomb, 37, 171, 174
Australia, 36
Australopithecenes, 106
Avoidance-and-diversion technique, 26, 34-38, 82

B

Baldwin, James, 158-9
Bantu, 56, 63
Barnett, Ross R., 166
Bean, Bennet, 52
Benedict, Ruth, 21-23
Bennett, E. L., 113
Biasutti, Renato, 29
Bible, 149

Biology of the Race Problem, 3, 42-43, 65n
Bloch, Charles, 75
Boas, Franz, 16-20, 23, 25-26, 29, 34, 41, 67, 69-71, 73
Bolivia, 47n
Bolton, J. S., 52
Brain, comparative anatomy of, in alligator, 52, 125; in ape, 51, 55; in dog, 51; in Eskimo, 101; in Neanderthal man, 102; in porpoise, 82, 105-6; in rabbit, 50; in rat, 113-4; in White and Negro, 4, 48-53, 55, 82-85, 103, 107; comparative electrophysiology of White and Negro, 55-56; comparative kinesthetic maturation rates of, 55, 97-99; importance of frontal lobes of, 49-50; loss of cells of, 102
Brazil, 110
Briggs vs. Elliott, 71
British Journal of Statistical Psychology, 58n
British Medical Journal, 84
Brodmann, K., 50n
Broken Hill specimen, 101, 109
Brooke, Edward, 126
Brotherhood, 7, 144, 152
Brown vs. Board of Education of Topeka, 36, 69, 70-71, 75, 120, 139, 141-3
Burt, Cyril, 58n, 71, 81
Business leaders, U.S., 148, 162-3
Buswell, James O., 43n

C

Cahn, Edmond, 141-3
Canella, Mario, 29
Cannibalism, 15, 170
Capital, 16n

186